Kim & Mary,

Thanks so much for your love and support!

May your ministry continue to grow and spread into new territories!

All the Best.

Carl

150 DAYS OF PEACE

DEVOTIONAL & JOURNAL

OVER 4 MONTHS of daily exercises and encouragement that creates a life of **abundant peace**, **clarity**, **& harmony**

CALVIN WITCHER

Witcher Publishing Group

This book may be purchased in bulk for educational, business, fundraising, or sales promotional use. For Information, please email info@witcherpublishing.com

Publishing consultation, support, design, and composition by Witcher Publishing Group. **www.witcherpublishing.com**.

Library of Congress Cataloging-in-Publication Data

Trade Paperback ISBN: 978-0-9971151-4-7
Trade Hardback ISBN: 978-0-9971151-5-4
E-book ISBN: 978-0-9971151-3-0

Because of the dynamic nature of the Internet, any web addresses or links contained in this book may have changed since publication and may no longer be valid. The views expressed in this work are solely those of the author and do not necessarily reflect the views of the publisher, and the publisher hereby disclaims any responsibility for them.

Witcher Publishing Group - rev. date: 09/15/2016

Witcher Publishing Group
Visit WitcherPublishing.com

A Special Thanks
& Exclusive Gift

&

JUST FOR YOU

As a thank you for purchasing *150 Days of Peace – Devotional & Journal*, **I would like to give you a special gift**?

Would that be ok?

I'd like to give you **FREE ACCESS** to the online companion videos (Valued at $30) just to say THANK YOU! You will have access **FOREVER** to the videos so be sure to take advantage of this today.

The videos are a great companion to help support your journey of peace. I understand that sometimes you may not have time to stop and write in your devotional and journal, so this is a way that you can continue your growth at your convenience!

Again, this is **COMPLETELY FREE** for you for purchasing *150 Days of Peace – Devotional & Journal*.

To redeem your gift, just visit **www.150DaysofPeace.com**
and enter the promo code: **BookPromoVideos**

*Again, thank you very much for choosing to live a life of peace
and partnering with me in that process.*

Dedication

శ్రీ

This devotional is dedicated
to my grandmother,
Stella Mae Witcher,
who continually taught me
the value and virtue of
pursing peace.

May you continue to
rest in peace,
rise in power, and
reveal in purpose.

Foreword

బ

Calvin Witcher's *150 Days of Peace – Devotional & Journal* is a healthy donation into your soul's investment fund. True to his direct, yet compassionate teaching style in his first book, *Parenting with Pieces*, his second offering, *150 Days of Peace*, is a stirring soul-map for the conscious adventurer.

In my time with this book, I discovered a unique way of creating a conscious arrival to each new day - and yes, that has brought me even more joy!

Meditation is my daily practice. As an intuitive counselor and healing facilitator, it is my business and my passion. I remember the beginning of my meditation journey and how valuable a guide like this one would have been, along my path. It is a golden egg for those who are seeking greater nourishment in their mindfulness practice and meditation mastery, without the confusing process that can keep us discouraged and out of touch with our progress.

Perspective change and attitude shift are accessible through Calvin's seamless ability to use spirit-coded language to pull out inner empowerment and bring forth conscious guidance. In my time knowing Calvin, we have shared the divine attitude of peace. I am confident that the knowledge and guided facilitation in this book will be a beautiful and timely gift for those who crack it open.

Take a deep breath;
close your eyes;
and envision the best version of your Self.

Your walk into that embodiment will be greatly impacted by your choice to follow this guide.

Calvin's wisdom and candor comes from a place of experience, a place of enthusiasm, and a place of love. This book is a reflection of his very heart for the healing of humanity - which starts right here at the foot of our own journeys.

– **BUDDHA-NOAH ALVAREZ**
Universal Preacher, Meditation
and Mindfulness Master Facilitator

Introduction

ॐ

How do we form new habits? The simple answer is practice. Many of us desire to get rid of negative habits and create new positive habits. Whatever we desire to see in our life, we must put the structure in place to support our needs and wants.

This daily devotional and journal is designed to guide you into a thriving and transformed life. This guide contains over four months of daily exercises and encouragement that creates a life of abundant peace, clarity, and harmony.

So, why did I create *150 Days of Peace – Devotional & Journal*? I believe most people, like you, want to change their life for the better and they only need tools to help facilitate the progress. I want to help in that process. If you ask the general public how long it takes to break a habit and create a new one, on average, you'll get answers ranging from 21-30 days.

There's no shortage of books, apps and teachers suggesting ways to form a new habit and much of this information is based on the assumption that all you need is 21 days. This magical number comes from a widely popular book, which was written in 1960, called *Psycho-Cybernetics* by Maxwell Maltz. Maltz, a plastic surgeon, noticed many of his patients seemed to take about 21 days to get used to their new faces.[i]

Interesting enough, forming a new habit is very much like putting on a "new face." Isn't it? When you are learning to create a new norm, it can look and feel like you're not yourself. You can feel like a different person. And, when the process is fully experienced, it can leave you feeling like you are a completely different person altogether. Who you "used to be" seems like a stranger and the negative patterns you used to have may seem foreign also.

According to a 2009 study, by researchers from University College London, the time it takes to form a habit is not as clear as previously thought. Phillippa Lally and colleagues investigated the new habits of 96 people over the space of 12 weeks. In their study, they observed how long it took for individuals to reach a limit of self-reported automaticity (that is performing an action automatically). They found that the average time it takes for a new habit to stick is actually 66 days; and, individual times varied from 18 to a staggering 254 days.[ii]

So, what's the take-away? It may take you at least two months to form a new habit, so don't get discouraged if you see little progress after a few weeks. For this reason, this devotional provides over 4 months, or 150 days, to help you create a new lifestyle of peace. Keep moving forward and you'll experience lasting change.

The truth is that we are all different, and consequently the time is takes one individual to form a new habit can be drastically different for another. No matter how long it takes you to grow, I encourage you to find peace your own process. I believe this will greatly help support your progress.

Peace is not an end goal but an evolving one. While peace can have multiple meanings, it is undeniable when we experience it.

My challenge, encouragement, and recommendation to you is to use this devotional as a way of tracking and celebrating your growth. This devotional is part informational, part instructional, and also part journal. There are daily quotes, following a brief summation and a thought to help frame your day. There are questions that I encourage you to complete and exercises that I encourage you to engage in.

Here's to a wonderful journey of self-discovery. I believe in you.

DAY 1 – LOVE YOURSELF

"You yourself, as much as anybody in the entire universe, deserve your love and affection."
– Buddha –

Giving love to others is admirable, but do you know how to love yourself? Many have been taught that to love one's self is selfish and to be avoided at all costs. This view of loving yourself is misguided. True love for yourself is the foundation from which you can give love to others. If you are conflicted or harboring self-hate, then you will only give that hate to those around you.

So, as we are giving love to others, we also need to focus on giving love and affection to ourselves. Only when we know how to truly love ourselves, can we better know how to give love and affection to other people.

Questions:

1.   **What is your honest view of loving yourself?**

_____

_____

_____

2.   **What are ways in which you excel at showing yourself love?**

_____

_____

_____

3.   **What are three tangible actions that you can show love to yourself today?**

_____

_____

_____

JOURNAL:

DAY 2 – HAVE CLEARLY DEFINED GOALS

"In absence of clearly defined goals, we become strangely loyal to performing daily acts of trivia."
– Robert Heinlein –

Today your challenge is to have clearly defined goals. Oftentimes, when we don't have clearly defined goals we get caught up in the little things; the small things that don't really help us accomplish our goals. Without clearly defined goals, we will not find fulfillment. I am sure you know what I am talking about. You know when you are picking at issues that don't really matter. You know when you are pushing against situations just to prove a point.

When you find yourself seeking out trivial things, stop and ask yourself why you are doing this. Could it be that you simply don't have a clear objective for the moment? Ask yourself what you really want, and then ask yourself if what you are doing will bring about your desired goal. Don't get caught up in the trivial things. You will only suffer frustration. So today, I want you to focus on defining your goals. Start with the goals for the day, and break those down to morning goals and afternoon goals. Then stick to actions that will peacefully fulfill those goals.

Questions:

1.   **What are you goals for today?**

_____

_____

_____

2.   **What actions will bring life to those goals?**

_____

_____

_____

JOURNAL: _____

_____

3.　　　**What are three steps that you will choose to keep yourself on task today?**

_____

_____

JOURNAL:

_____

_____

_____

_____

_____

_____

_____

_____

_____

_____

_____

_____

_____

_____

_____

_____

_____

_____

_____

DAY 3 - PRAY

"When the world pushes you to your knees, you're in the perfect position to pray."
– Rumi –

Do you feel like you are carrying the world on your shoulders? Has the weight of your problems and responsibilities brought you to your knees? If so, then you have an opportunity to pray. What do I mean? Prayer is simply asking for help. If you have a God that you believe in, then pray to your deity. If you have a friend you can reach out to for support, then ask for help.

Sometimes the help we really need comes from outside ourselves, but sometimes we know that we can look for help within ourselves. If you know you have the answers within you, then take the time to stop what you're doing, be still, and listen for the answers. Wherever your help comes from, receive the help. Don't be afraid to ask. You are not a failure because you need assistance. Everyone needs help at some point along the way. Ask for help, realize that you don't have to carry the weight of the world on your back, and then move forward with renewed encouragement.

Questions:

1. **Who do you "pray" to?**

_____

_____

_____

2. **What help do you need?**

_____

_____

_____

3. **Have you asked for help?**

_____

_____

DAY 4 – LIFE AND DEATH

"The boundaries which divide life from death are at best shadowy and vague. Who shall say where one ends, and the other begins?"

– Edgar Alan Poe –

All of us are having experiences that are giving us life, or possibly giving us death. Every moment of your day is playing into the creation that is YOU. Everything has a purpose. Even those moments that seem like a "death" are useful. Death is merely the closing of one chapter, and life is the beginning of another. This is why sometimes we don't know where one ends and the other begins. Both are necessary.

So, if you experience the feeling of death or loss today, remind yourself that out of death comes life. Keep a balanced perspective. Enjoy each moment and find appreciation in everything.

Questions:
1.   **What situations yesterday felt like death?**

_____

_____

_____

2.   **What situations yesterday felt like life?**

_____

_____

_____

3.   **What good came out of yesterday's death experiences?**

_____

_____

_____

JOURNAL:

4.   What good came out of yesterday's life experiences?

_____

_____

_____

5.   What connections (if any) did the death/life experiences have?

_____

_____

_____

6.   What are two physical actions you can take today to keep a balanced
        perspective?

_____

_____

JOURNAL: _____

_____

_____

_____

_____

_____

_____

_____

_____

_____

_____

_____

_____

150 DAYS OF
PEACE

"Believe you can and you're halfway there."
– Theodore Roosevelt –

Sometimes we stop right before we get our breakthrough. Sometimes we stop right before we reach our goal. No one said that your path was going to be easy. However, your goals will succeed with persistence. Yes, you may change strategies or find clarity through your mistakes, but in the end you will reach your goal if you don't quit. And, an underlining belief in yourself today is what it is going to take.

Your mind is a powerful tool. What you say to yourself, about yourself, drastically shapes your experience. Find or re-find your goals today. Then, once you have those goals in focus, believe you can fulfill them. Your belief in yourself has propelled you halfway toward your goals.

Questions:

1.   What is one positive belief you have about yourself?

_____

_____

_____

2.   What is one positive belief you have about your goals?

_____

_____

_____

3.   What are two actions you will do today to move you closer to your goals?

_____

_____

_____

JOURNAL: _____

_____

DAY 6 – IMPROVE THE PRESENT

"Look not mournfully into the past, it comes not back again. Wisely improve the present, it is thine. Go forth to meet the shadowy future without fear and with a manly heart."
– Henry Wadsworth Longfellow –

Try to avoid looking back in the past. The past is done. The best thing to do for you and your future is to take mindful stock in everything you are doing right now in this moment. Choose balanced healthy solutions right now. As you make good decisions, you improve your future and your past becomes obsolete. I know this may be hard for you to do if you are a person who struggles with letting go of the past. But, this piece of advice is priceless. Do not get stuck repeating, in your mind, the story of your past.

Allow for the wisdom that came from those experiences, and then choose to do something for yourself in the NOW. Likewise, do not look too far out into the future. The future is "shadowy" for a reason. There are many things about your future that depend on your choice right here–right now. So stop. Breathe. Look around you. See yourself here. Take as long as you need. Now, from this place, take action.

Questions:

1. **What story about the past do you want to let go?**

_____

_____

_____

2. **What story about the future creates fear?**

_____

_____

_____

JOURNAL:

_____

_____

3.   What is actually happening right now?

_____

_____

_____

4.   What parts about those two stories have nothing to do with this moment?

_____

_____

_____

5.   What will you say to yourself if you see yourself stressing about your past or future?

_____

_____

JOURNAL:
_____

_____

_____

_____

_____

_____

_____

_____

_____

_____

_____

_____

_____

150 DAYS OF PEACE

"Success consists of going from failure to failure without loss of enthusiasm."
– Winston Churchill –

Everyone goes through failures or challenging times. I hope this message finds you doing well, but if you are struggling—take heart. Remember you are going to succeed in your life no matter what. There is nothing that can take you off the path you purposed to follow. Often you will look back with greater understanding and appreciation for the moments that felt like failure. You will understand that those "failures" were turns in the road that directed you to tangible success. No, failure doesn't feel good. But, learn to embrace failure without losing your joy.

Find something good in what you went through. This, in and of itself, constitutes a level of success. You will find yourself rising above your circumstances and glimpsing the bigger picture. I know you may not feel like you are successful in this moment, but you are. Take every failure as an opportunity to grow. And, if you are feeling successful right now, then be grateful and remember this message for the future.

Questions:

1.   **How are you doing?**

_____

_____

_____

2.   **What is going well for you?**

_____

_____

_____

JOURNAL:

_____

_____

_____

3. **What are you grateful for?**

_____

_____

4. **What are three things you have learned from your most recent failure?**

_____

_____

_____

5. **What action will you take today as a result of the lessons you learned?**

_____

_____

JOURNAL:

_____

_____

_____

_____

_____

_____

_____

_____

_____

_____

_____

_____

_____

_____

DAY 8 – ADJUST YOUR EXPECTATIONS

"We must be willing to relinquish the life we've planned, so as to have the life that is waiting for us."
– Joseph Campbell –

This is simple. Don't get so invested in your plans that you can't enjoy the life you already have. Don't be so rigid in your plans that you are unable to make adjustments. Being inflexible is how you get stuck. Plans are valid as long as they prove themselves useful.

When your plans do not fit your goals, they need to be adjusted. Or, when your goals change, your plans need to change with those goals. Plans are just tools to get us what we want. Nothing is set in stone. So, first of all enjoy what you already have. You have done great so far. Next, relax. Be ok with plans changing. You will be fine no matter what happens.

Questions:

1.   What is one plan that is getting in your way?

_____

_____

_____

2.   How can you change that plan to better fit your goal?

_____

_____

_____

3.   What are two things you like about your life?

_____

_____

_____

DAY 9 – KNOWLEDGE BRINGS FORGIVENESS

"The more a man knows, the more he forgives."
– Catherine the Great –

Real knowledge comes through experience, and through experience comes true understanding. How many times have we said, "I would never do that", or "I don't see how anyone could...?" Maybe you said that you would never repeat something a parent did only to find yourself years later saying or doing the very thing you promised never to do. It is in those moments that we find understanding in the situation. We understand how a person could get to the point in question.

We understand that we are as human as the next person. We find a sense of humility, and we are better able to listen to the experiences of others. What is it we understand? We understand that no moment is as we first understood it. Experience teaches us the details of an event. Understanding, empathizing, forgiveness; these are a few gifts that experiential knowledge brings us. Remember, we are all going through this journey of life together. Forgive yourself and then forgive others.

Questions:

1. **Who do you need to forgive?**

_____

_____

_____

2. **How do you need to express this forgiveness?**

_____

_____

_____

3. **What are you going to do today to put forgiveness into action?**

_____

_____

_____

150 DAYS OF PEACE

> ## "Life is a pure flame, and we live by an invisible sun within us."
> ### – Sir Thomas Brown –

Remember today that you have a light inside you. That light is helping guide you wherever you might go. Enjoy this light no matter what you face. I am not just talking to the bubbly personalities out there. I am also including those darker brooding souls. We all have that eternal spark that gives us drive and purpose to follow our dreams.

Maybe you need to fan the flames of your light. Then do so. You have a pure flame inside you. Imagine all the force of the sun housed inside your body. This is you. You are powerful. Go shine your light.

Questions:

1. **What sparks your interest?**

_____

_____

_____

2. **What makes you smile?**

_____

_____

_____

3. **What can you do for someone else to put a smile on their face today?**

_____

_____

_____

JOURNAL:

_____

_____

150 DAYS OF
PEACE

"Good fortune and bad are equally necessary to man, to fit him to meet the contingencies of this life."
– French Proverb –

Everything we go through is about balance. When we go through the "bad" times it only gives us more reverence for the "good" times. Remember that your bad times always turn into good times. So, keep perspective. Try not to run from problems.

Take a moment, get yourself into a safe space, and reflect. Ask yourself, "What is this moment teaching me?" "What can I use moving forward to be a better person and create a better life?" Be thankful for the clarity that your dark times bring and rejoice in the good fortune you will receive along your way.

Questions:
1.   **What is one bad thing that happened to you today?**

_____

_____

_____

2.   **How can you use your bad experience moving forward?**

_____

_____

_____

3.   **What is one good thing that happened to you today?**

_____

_____

_____

JOURNAL:

_____

_____

4.   How can you use your good experience moving forward?

_____

_____

JOURNAL: _____

_____

_____

_____

_____

_____

_____

_____

_____

_____

_____

_____

_____

_____

_____

_____

_____

_____

_____

_____

DAY 12 – ACT LIKE SOMEONE'S WATCHING

"Govern thy life and thoughts as if the whole world were to see the one, and read the other."
– Thomas Fuller –

We perform better and do better when we know someone is watching us. This is called, "The Observer Effect." What if someone was watching you right now? How would you feel? What action might you change? If someone were to read your thoughts right now, how would they react? Would you be proud of the thoughts you have? The point of this exercise is transparency of soul.

Sometimes we fool ourselves into thinking that we are ok when, in truth, we have little bits of anger, bitterness, or fear tucked away in the recesses of our mind. So, when you see a thought cross your mind that is anything but love, ask yourself what you might be harboring. Ask yourself if this is who you want to be.

What would you change if you knew someone was watching you? Would you be proud of yourself if these ideas were written down for the world to read? What would you like others to see? What do you want others to read about you? Thinking about this will help you perform better and do better. My challenge to you is this—live and think in such a way that will uplift you. I know you can.

Questions:

1. **Who inspires you?**

_____

_____

_____

2. **What positive attributes do you admire in them?**

_____

_____

_____

JOURNAL:

_____

_____

3.   **What thoughts will help you be the person you want to be?**

_____

_____

_____

4.   **What positive action will you do today to make this a reality?**

_____

_____

JOURNAL:
_____

_____

_____

_____

_____

_____

_____

_____

_____

_____

_____

_____

_____

_____

_____

_____

150 DAYS OF PEACE

> ## "Believe in yourself! Have faith in your abilities! Without a humble but reasonable confidence in your own powers you cannot be successful or happy."
> ### – Norman Vincent Peale –

Believe in yourself. Have faith in your abilities. No matter what you face today, you have the power to find solutions. You have the power to be happy. You have the ability to handle each moment with grace and confidence. Remind yourself how great you are and how far you have already come.

Questions:

1.   **Name three areas where you feel powerful.**

_____

_____

_____

2.   **What are your greatest abilities?**

_____

_____

_____

3.   **How are you going to use your strengths today?**

_____

_____

_____

4.   **Smile.**

_____

_____

_____

150 DAYS OF
PEACE

"Aspiring minds must sometimes sustain loss."
– Plato –

People who have gained the most have often lost the most at one point in their life. If and when you find yourself at a loss, remember this is not the end of your story. Honor those times and use them as tools. Remind yourself that you are becoming greater through this loss. I am not minimizing loss. Any loss great or small is painful. But, we can learn and grow through each experience and come out a better person.

Today, if you have a loss, you are not alone. You are positioned to have great gains in the future.

Questions:

1.   **What have you lost?**

_____

_____

_____

2.   **How might you (or have you) grown through this experience?**

_____

_____

_____

3.   **How can this loss be turned into a gain?**

_____

_____

_____

4.   **What action will you take today to demonstrate your personal growth?**

_____

_____

150 DAYS OF
PEACE

DAY 15 – LEARN TO BE CONTENT

"Fortify yourself with contentment, for this is an impregnable fortress."
– Epictetus –

Contentment is a powerful building tool. Learning to be content or at peace with all things is vital. So the challenge today is simple - be content. One way to start this is to list the things you are thankful for. Focus on things you like and the things that are working for you. This way, when trouble comes, it cannot penetrate you. Watch your conversations to see if they build contentment into your life or if they are tearing down the fortress contentment brings. Choose actions that demonstrate a thankful spirit. Your life is full of wonderful things. Take the time to notice them.

Questions:

1.   **What are you thankful for?**

_____

_____

_____

2.   **How are you going to show your contentment today?**

_____

_____

JOURNAL: _____

_____

_____

_____

_____

_____

_____

DAY 16 – WHAT YOU PUT IN IS WHAT YOU GET OUT

"Life is something like a trumpet. If you don't put anything in, you don't get anything out."
– WC. Handy –

Whatever you put in is exactly what you get out. This is true with any instrument. The same is true with your life. Life is not happening to you, but YOU will happen to life. In order to enjoy the harmonies of life, you have to put great notes into life. You need to pick "notes" carefully and with purpose. Today's question is, "What are you putting into your life?" What song are you trying to play and are you picking the notes and rhythm that is creating that song? You are the variable here. Everything else is just a tool. Don't blame the instrument for being out of tune. Let's not fuss about being off tempo.

When you see or hear yourself producing chaotic music, STOP. Tune things up. Find the note that fits the song. Practice. You will then create a song that everyone wants to hear. So today, go make some music. Play your song. Create the music you love.

Questions:

1.   **What do you want to get out of your life?**

_____

_____

_____

2.   **What are you putting into your life?**

_____

_____

_____

3.   **What choices do you need to "tune up" today?**

_____

_____

"The only place where your dream becomes impossible is in your own thinking."
– Robert H Schuller –

Your dreams are possible. Your dreams can come true. Are you limiting your future through fearful thoughts? One of the keys to fulfilling your dreams is to remove your limitations. What are some of the things that limit you? Is it a place, job, or relationship? Ask yourself if the limiting reasons you have are true? Why can't you do what you want? We all have choices we can make.

When we allow a person or circumstance to limit our dreams we are either thinking too small, or we are using the situation as an excuse for not going after our dreams. I am not asking you to get rid of every challenge. I am asking you to allow the "limit" to become a launching pad for success. Nothing is standing in your way. Nothing is against you. Free yourself. Focus on the possibilities. Let the "limit" redirect you to a better solution.

Questions:
1.   What is your "limit" today?

_____

_____

_____

2.   How will you redirect your thoughts about this limit?

_____

_____

_____

3.   What is one action you can take to move past this limit?

_____

_____

_____

DAY 18 – CHOOSE A FOCUS

"He who would arrive at the appointed end must follow a single road and not wander through many ways."
– Seneca –

Your life must be focused on a single path. I did not say there is only one path. However, you need to follow one path. If you were driving and tried to follow multiple roads at the same time, you would never get to your destination. You must follow one road at a time. Yes, there may be many roads that lead to the same place, but you must choose one of those roads to follow. Doing anything less will either split your energies or keep you spinning in the same place. Choose a focus and follow a single path today. This will bring you clarity. This will bring you mastery.

Questions:

1.   **What is your focus for today?**

_____

_____

_____

2.   **What actions line up with today's focus?**

_____

_____

_____

3.   **What can wait for another day?**

_____

_____

_____

JOURNAL: _____

_____

_____

4.   How will you kindly redirect yourself if you see yourself get off focus?

_____

_____

JOURNAL:
_____
_____
_____
_____
_____
_____
_____
_____
_____
_____
_____
_____
_____
_____
_____
_____
_____
_____
_____
_____
_____

"Nothing is predestined; The obstacles of your past can become the gateways that lead to new beginnings."
– Ralph Blum –

Nothing is set in stone. Everything you have gone through has set you up for this particular moment. Everything you face today is setting your foundation for your future. Relax. Let go of rigidity. You are always growing, changing, and developing. Each of today's moments are subject to change. You are the one who can bring about this change. You have all the tools necessary to create the day you want. Let each obstacle be your gateway and enjoy the journey.

Questions:

1. **What happens when you don't get your way?**

_____

_____

_____

2. **What new perspective will you have today?**

_____

_____

_____

3. **How can you show flexibility and still keep moving toward your dreams?**

_____

_____

_____

JOURNAL:

_____

_____

_____

"Life is a succession of lessons which must be lived to be understood."
– Ralph Waldo Emerson –

Are you the kind of person who lives for the weekend? Do you find yourself complaining at work that the day is long? Are you rushing to finish a task so you can get to the "good" parts of life? I want you to slow down. Remember today is a lesson. Rushing through life will cause you to repeat life. Avoiding certain situations in your life will only allow those same situations to show up later. There is no end. There is no understanding of anything without going through the process. There are no life cheat sheets.

Learn from today the lessons that are yours. You don't have to repeat today's lesson.

Questions:

1.   **What are you trying to rush?**

_____

_____

_____

2.   **What are you trying to avoid?**

_____

_____

_____

3.   **At the end of this day write down three new things that you have learned.**

_____

_____

_____

JOURNAL:

DAY 21 – TODAY IS A NEW BEGINNING

"Today is a new beginning, a chance to turn your failures into achievements and your sorrows into so goods. No room for excuses."
– Joel Brown –

Live life without excuses. Today is a new day. You have an opportunity to try better and do better. Yesterday is gone and tomorrow is not here. Today is your moment. Today is the gift you have. Shake off any of the stress and tension that you are holding onto. Literally get up and shake it off.

Take a deep breath. Calm your mind and trust your inner being. You can achieve everything you want today.

Questions:

1.   What is new about today?

_____

_____

_____

2.   What excuses will you let go of?

_____

_____

_____

3.   What achievements will you make today?

_____

_____

_____

JOURNAL:

_____

_____

DAY 22 – THE SECRET OF SUCCESS

"In everything, the ends well defined are the secret of durable success."
– Victor Cousins –

I know you want success. But what does your success look like? Your version of success will most likely be different from mine. So, have you thought about what you will think, feel, or experience once you have reached your success? Without a clear definition of your particular kind of success you might miss it.

You might always be searching and yet never find your dream. So today, create a defined end to one of your goals. This allows you to take actionable steps to achieving this goal and it also allows you to celebrate when you do reach this goal. Do this with each of your goals and even break up your goals into smaller goals. Then pay attention to your day and see how many small successes you have.

Questions:
1.   **What is your big goal?**

_____

_____

_____

2.   **What are the smaller goals that go into reaching your big goal?**

_____

_____

_____

3.   **What are four actions today that will help you reach a small goal?**

_____

_____

_____

JOURNAL:

150 DAYS OF
PEACE

"Do not anticipate trouble, or worry about what may never happen. Keep in the sunlight."
– Benjamin Franklin –

Today keep in the sunlight. The sunlight I am talking about are those positive thoughts and actions that allow you to grow and thrive. Stay in the mental and physical spaces where your spirit is uplifted. This does not mean trouble never comes. Let's be real—it does. But there is no need to anticipate trouble. Doing so only exacerbates them. It's better to have trouble find you when you are in a healthy and positive state of mind, than for trouble to find you already down and discouraged. And honestly, aren't most of your troubles fake?

How many worries of yesterday actually came true? And what troubles were brought on because you worried about them. So, my point is stay in the sunlight. There you will receive everything you want and more than you need.

Questions:
1. **What fear do you have today?**

_____

_____

_____

2. **What would the opposite (or sunlight) of that fear be? Focus on this.**

_____

_____

_____

3. **What are two actions that will help you stay in your sunlight?**

_____

_____

_____

DAY 24 – CHANGE IS NECESSARY

"Change is not merely necessary to life, it is life."
– Alvin Toffler –

I want you to be effective in every area of your life. This means that you will change. You are not perfect in all things. That is ok. You can change that. And, even those areas where you have achieved a level of success, you will want to develop even more. Again, change is going to come. Your life is about change. So embrace change. Play with change. Enjoy change. Although change is sometimes uncomfortable, change is a necessary part of life. Learn to understand and appreciate changes as they come. Change will always be a part of your journey.

Questions:

1.   **How do you feel about change?**

_____

_____

_____

2.   **What do you want to change?**

_____

_____

_____

3.   **How are you going to make that change happen today?**

_____

_____

_____

JOURNAL:

_____

_____

_____

_____

DAY 25 – SURMOUNTING FEAR

"He has not learned the lesson of life who does not every day surmount a fear."
– Ralph Waldo Emerson –

The purpose of fear is to drive us to a place of safety where we can grow and thrive. When you are in a state of fear, all you are focused on is getting to safety. Fear is a great tool to keep us alive. However, fear by itself will always try to keep you in the same place. Fear does not want you to grow, it wants to protect you. Growth, at any level, asks us to explore areas that seem unsafe. This will always cause us fear. So, I want you to be able to use your fear, and if needed—conquer your fear.

Learn the lesson of life which is to continually grow. And as you grow, encourage yourself that the fears of today are the comforts of tomorrow.

Questions:

1.   **What do you want today?**

_____

_____

_____

2.   **What fear comes to mind that would keep you from your goal?**

_____

_____

_____

3.   **How are you going to surmount this fear?**

_____

_____

_____

JOURNAL: _____

_____

DAY 26 – BE THE GREATEST

"I am the greatest. I said that even before I knew I was."
– Muhammad Ali –

Do you know how great you are? Do you understand that you are great before you have the proof of your greatness? You are powerful. You are capable. You are uniquely gifted for the tasks in front of you today. Encourage yourself. Love yourself. And proclaim to yourself that you are the greatest. Why should you do this? You are what you think. You are the substance of the energy that you emit and surround yourself with.

Want to be the greatest? Be great in your thoughts and beliefs. From those forces of energy will flow tangible proof of who you are.

Questions:

1.   **Who are you?**

_____

_____

_____

2.   **Have you told yourself who you are today?**

_____

_____

_____

3.   **Tell yourself something positive you have no proof of and keep repeating this to yourself throughout your day.**

_____

_____

_____

JOURNAL:

DAY 27 – MAKE YOUR OWN LUCK

"We make our fortunes, and we call them fate."
– Earl of Beaconsfield –

Chance will bring you nothing. Luck does not exist. Do not wait today for something or someone to drop an answer into your lap. You make your own luck. Give yourself your own answer. Seek out the things you want and you will find them. Put the work into this day, moment by moment, and you will see results. By living a life of intent you will step into your destiny and what once was your fate will become your intended creation.

Questions:

1. **What is one thing you have been waiting on others to do for you?**

_____

_____

_____

2. **How can you find the solution yourself?**

_____

_____

_____

JOURNAL:

_____

_____

_____

_____

_____

_____

_____

_____

_____

DAY 28 – LIGHT DRIVES OUT DARKNESS

"Darkness cannot drive out darkness;
only light can do that.
Hate cannot drive out hate;
only love can do that."
– Dr. Martin Luther King Jr. –

It is easy to fight fire with fire, but all you will get is more fire. If it is change that you want, then you need to find the opposite of the problem. Light and dark are opposites. An answer to the dark room is a lit candle. An answer to the burning sun is a drawn curtain. Whatever you are having a problem with today, find the opposite of that problem, and there you will start finding solutions. Remember to do all things in balance and you will find your way.

Questions:

1.   **What is your biggest challenge you face today?**

_____

_____

_____

2.   **What energy would be the opposite of this challenge?**

_____

_____

_____

3.   **What action would bring you closer to a solution?**

_____

_____

_____

JOURNAL:

_____

_____

150 DAYS OF
PEACE

"The rays of happiness, like those of light, are colorless when unbroken."
– Henry W. Longfellow –

Within light you find many colors. However, only when light is broken up do you enjoy its spectrum. Prisms are prime examples. Applied to happiness, this principle gives great insight and perspective to challenges that you face. How often have you felt broken by a situation or a relationship? It is in those moments (specific and "colorful" parts) of happiness that transform your life. Because of your broken moments, you are and have been becoming a more colorful and beautiful person. Today, if you come across a challenge, use it to find a new color; a new aspect of happiness. You are beautiful no matter what.

Questions:

1. **What is a broken place in your life?**

_____

_____

_____

2. **How can happiness be shown in this situation?**

_____

_____

_____

3. **How is this new form of happiness different from your previous experiences?**

_____

_____

_____

JOURNAL:

_____

_____

DAY 30 – HOW TO LIVE TO PURPOSE

"The great and glorious masterpiece of man is to know how to live to purpose."
– Michel de Montaigne –

I want you to master living a purpose driven life. Living a life of purpose is understanding that you are the master of your own journey. You are putting the pieces together. You are sculpting and painting your own masterpiece. You may not know exactly what shape your art will take in the beginning, but over time you will start to see your masterpiece take shape. Great art takes time and dedication. Encourage yourself today to keep honing your craft. Keep practicing and allow for your art to develop. Take pride in each step along the way.

Questions:

1.   **What are you practicing today?**

_____

_____

_____

2.   **What creation can you already celebrate?**

_____

_____

_____

3.   **What part of your craft would you like to improve?**

_____

_____

_____

JOURNAL:

_____

_____

_____

DAY 31 – LIFE GOES ON

"In three words I can sum up everything I know about life. It goes on."
– Robert Frost –

Life goes on. Nothing stops. Will you continue to go on? Will you continue through your struggles and challenges or will you stop? The truth is, not even you can stop life's journey. One way, or the other, it moves forward. So too must you. I know there may be moments when you feel that you can't go on. You might have suffered a great loss, or are simply weary in your everyday tasks. Take heart. Breath. Find rejuvenation. But do not quit. Keep going. I know you can.

Questions:

1.   How have you kept going during a past challenge?

_____

_____

_____

2.   What will you tell yourself today if you have a challenge?

_____

_____

_____

3.   What will you do today to rejuvenate yourself?

_____

_____

_____

JOURNAL:
_____

_____

_____

DAY 32 – ENJOY SUCCESS

"There are two things to aim at in life; first to get what you want, and after that to enjoy it. Only the wisest of mankind has achieved the second."
– Logan Pearsall Smith –

Are you constantly asking for more? Great! Keep wanting to grow and expand. But today, I want you to enjoy something you have received. Look around you and find joy in what you have already accomplished. Remind yourself of the points in your life where what you have now seemed like a dream. Congratulate yourself on what you made happen. Its ok. Work will be waiting for you. Today, give yourself a break and enjoy yourself.

Questions:

1.   **What two things have you wanted and received?**

_____

_____

_____

2.   **When is the last time you enjoyed those things?**

_____

_____

_____

3.   **What are you going to enjoy today?**

_____

_____

_____

JOURNAL:

_____

_____

_____

DAY 33 – DEALING WITH STUMBLING BLOCKS

"The difference between stumbling blocks and stepping stones is how you use them."
– Unknown –

If you feel like you have a stumbling block in your life, I want you to change your perspective just a little bit and see the stumbling block as a stepping stone. Instead of seeing an obstacle, look at what opportunity has been given you. Most of the time, we complain about a situation because the opportunity wasn't planned by us. So, because we hadn't anticipated the opportunity, we view it as an obstacle and miss the important lessons or new help life has brought us.

My favorite personal example is the time I asked for more patience and then found myself complaining because I had to wait in line. You know exactly what I am talking about. Allow your journey of life to unfold before you. All that you have asked is on its way to you. Everything you want will be yours. Embrace the moments that bring you what you want. Remind yourself that you did indeed ask for some part of each situation. Challenge yourself to uncover your stepping stones today.

Questions:
1.   **What is your biggest stumbling block?**

_____

_____

_____

2.   **What might be the hidden stepping stone in this situation?**

_____

_____

_____

3.   **What action can you take to use this stepping stone for your good?**

_____

_____

150 DAYS OF
PEACE

"A loving heart is the truest wisdom."
– Charles Dickens –

Fear does not allow us to make balanced choices. Love brings clarity and wisdom to each situation. Love allows us to see things as they really are. Today, I want you to take time to ask yourself the following question: Am I operating in fear or in love?

Questions:

1.   **What is motivating you in this moment – fear or love?**

_____

_____

_____

2.   **What thoughts will bring or keep you in love today?**

_____

_____

_____

3.   **How can you tangibly show love?**

_____

_____

JOURNAL:

_____

_____

_____

_____

_____

_____

DAY 35 – YOU ARE INVINCIBLE

"In the midst of winter, I found there was within me an invincible summer."
– Albert Careb –

Did you know you are invincible? Yes, you are an invincible soul and you are an invincible spirit. Winter is often associated with death and likewise summer with life. However, both winter and summer are necessary to our development. When you are in winter or the seemingly dead times of life, you might not feel so invincible. But just because it seems like there is little life during winter, doesn't mean that there aren't hints of summer or life right under the surface.

When you feel like you are in winter (either your own winter or the winter of others') look deep inside yourself—under the snow—and you will find that there is in you an everlasting summer or an everlasting life. You can maintain your invincibility during every season of life.

Questions:

1. **What season of life are you in?**

_____

_____

_____

2. **What signs of life can you see in yourself?**

_____

_____

_____

3. **How will you demonstrate your invincibility today?**

_____

_____

_____

DAY 36 – CHANGE YOUR THOUGHTS

"Change your thoughts and you change your world."
– Norman Vincent Peale –

Are you waiting for the world around you to change? You might want your relationships to change, your boss to change, the traffic to change; all these external things to change. In order for your external world to change, your internal world needs to change first. This starts with your thoughts.

Today, your challenge is to change one thought. Find an area of external life that you want to change. What is that one thing or person that you keep telling yourself needs to change in order for you to change. Now, flip your thinking about that person or subject. Instead of waiting for your external experience to change, you be the change first. Once you have done this, move on throughout your day. Get off the subject. If you continue to practice a changed thought about this subject, you will see this subject change in the next few days or weeks. Try it. It will change your world.

Questions:
1. **What do you want to change?**

_____

_____

_____

2. **How can you flip your perspective about this topic?**

_____

_____

_____

3. **How can you put into action your new perspective?**

_____

_____

_____

DAY 37 – PLAY THE ROLE OF YOUR LIFE

"Life is a play. It's not its length, but its performance that counts."
– Seneca –

Live life like a good play or good movie. You are the character in your own story. You know what kind of movies/plays thrill you or spark your interest. Those are usually the ones where the actors have played the roles to the fullest. You too, as the actor in your own story, want to play the role of your life—literally. This is your story. This is your role. You create your own character. Put your all into every part of the production from the rehearsal to the final curtain.

Every place you are and every experience you go through is a scene in the great epic story that is You. Enjoy being the star. Today, be all that you know you want to be. Create a story that is yours.

Questions:

1. **What is your story?**

_____

_____

_____

2. **How are you telling your message?**

_____

_____

_____

3. **What are three actions that will perfect your story?**

_____

_____

_____

JOURNAL:

DAY 38 – EVERYTHING IS AN OPPORTUNITY

"With everything that has happened to you, you can either feel sorry for yourself or treat what has happened as a gift. Everything is either an opportunity to grow or an obstacle to keep you from growing. You get to choose."
– Dr. Wayne W. Dyer –

Everything in your life is helping you grow. Nothing is truly an obstacle. A change of perspective is all that it takes to turn a negative situation into a gift. Is this always easy? Of course not. If it were, then everyone would do it. But, is a change of perspective possible? Absolutely! You will know you have really grown when the things that used to bother you no longer get to you. You have grown when you can say, "That's ok" and move forward. The work is the same. The choice is yours.

Questions:

1.   **In what area are you feeling sorry for yourself?**

_____

_____

_____

2.   **What is the gift in this situation?**

_____

_____

_____

3.   **How will you choose to use this gift and grow?**

_____

_____

_____

DAY 39 – NEVER DESPAIR

"Never despair."
– Horace –

Despair is simply to be without hope. Have you or are you going through a state of despair? Has this despair turned to depression? If so, I know it is hard for you to see the light at the end of the tunnel. But let me reassure you that there is light. Take it step by step. Try to find the little things that are good. Just one good thing in your life is enough to start the momentum of hope. And there is at least one good thing in your life.

Don't be afraid to reach out for help. You are not alone and you are not the only one who has gone through what you are going through. There is good in the world and there are good people who want to see you thrive.

Questions:

1.	**What is one good thing in your life?**

_____

_____

_____

2.	**How can you focus on this good thing today?**

_____

_____

_____

3.	**What person will you talk to today that might encourage you along your path?**

_____

_____

_____

JOURNAL:

_____

_____

150 DAYS OF PEACE

"To reach a port, we must sail – Sail, not tie an anchor – Sail, not drift."
– Franklin Roosevelt –

Today, don't put down your anchor and give up. Don't drift wherever the wind of life may blow. Be active and engaged in your life today. When you take ownership of your own ship (which is you) and you use the winds of life and the sea of opportunity for your own advantage, then you can sail. And, sail you will. You can achieve your goal or come to your destination. You have the force of all nature to use for your good. All things are for you and nothing is against you. Sail today and enjoy the trip.

Questions:

1. **What lifts you up?**

_____

_____

_____

2. **How can you use this positive momentum to keep you focused today?**

_____

_____

_____

3. **How will you remind yourself of your destination throughout the day?**

_____

_____

_____

JOURNAL: _____

_____

_____

_____

DAY 41 – ARRIVING AT THE GOAL

"Arriving at one goal is the starting point to another."
– John Dewey –

You will always have goals in your life. You will have something that you are always obtaining because this is the essence of life. The reaching of a goal is never the complete end. Yes, it is the end for that specific goal, but it is also an access point to for the start of a new goal. Have you ever felt let down when you reached a specific goal? Did you feel like there should be something more?

The feeling of being "let down" comes from not understanding this principle. There is no ultimate finishing line—if you will. Just the accomplishment of one goal and the start of another. So, celebrate your victories and know that with every new accomplishment comes a new perspective and a wonderful new beginning.

Questions:

1. **What achievement can you celebrate today?**

_____

_____

_____

2. **What is your next goal?**

_____

_____

_____

3. **What action will you take today to accomplish your new goal?**

_____

_____

_____

JOURNAL:

_____

_____

DAY 42 – HAPPINESS WILL ALWAYS FIND YOU

"Happiness often sneaks in through a door you didn't know you left open."
– John Barrymore –

Happiness will always find you. Have you tried seeking happiness? Have you been asked what makes you happy? Have you had a hard time answering such questions? That might be because true happiness is a by-product of living a full and purpose driven life. When you know who you are and embrace yourself with love—happiness follows. When you really understand your own value—happiness will follow. When you see yourself thriving—happiness sneaks up and hugs you.

When you embrace that you are a wonderful and powerful creature (you guessed it) happiness is there. So if you are feeling unhappy today, don't focus on trying to get happy. Go about your work—step by step. Take a deep breath and tell yourself everything is ok. Redirect your mind to areas where you can create forward movement. And, before you know it happiness will sneak in that door you left open.

Questions:

1.   What needs to get done today?

_____

_____

_____

2.   What will you get done in the next hour?

_____

_____

_____

3.   What do you want to get done in the next four hours?

_____

_____

_____

150 DAYS OF PEACE

"Life is like riding a bicycle. To keep your balance, you must keep moving."
– Albert Einstein –

When is the last time you rode a bike? No matter if you're an avid bike rider or haven't been on a bike in years, you know that you have to maintain balance and forward motion to stay on a bike. Life is the same. You can't have balance in your life, if you don't keep yourself moving. The moment you stop or hesitate is the moment you lose your balance. Those are the times you really struggle and life becomes difficult. You may even find yourself face down on the ground or slamming into a wall. So, today don't quit. Keep moving no matter what. You will find yourself traveling down your path with balance and speed.

Questions:

1.   **How can you move forward today in your goals?**

_____

_____

_____

2.   **What alternative action will you take, if you meet resistance?**

_____

_____

_____

JOURNAL: _____

_____

_____

_____

_____

_____

_____

150 DAYS OF
PEACE

"The gem cannot be polished without friction, nor man be perfected without trials."
– Danish Proverb –

You are a gem. You are valuable and of great worth. You are precious and priceless. Today, look yourself in the mirror and tell yourself that you are worth it and that you are intrinsically valuable. Get around people who reflect your worth back to you. Receive the love that others are giving to you because you deserve it. Don't worry about the places in your life that are causing you friction. It is because you are a costly gem that you are being polished and shined.

The world wants to see all the beauty that is inside you. When you feel 'cut' just remind yourself that you are being made into a stunning work of art. And, from your unique place and perspective in this world, you shine out just like a precious stone. Allow the process to happen, because we are all waiting to see the real you.

Questions:
1. **How will you remind yourself that you are worthy?**

_____

_____

_____

2. **Who will you speak to today that supports and reflects your worth?**

_____

_____

_____

3. **What do you need to allow (or release) so you can become more beautiful?**

_____

_____

_____

DAY 45 – COURAGE IS NEVER AFRAID

"The man of wisdom is never of two minds; the man of benevolence never worries; the man of courage is never afraid."
– Confucius –

You can't have your cake and eat it too. If you are going to be afraid, then there is no need to be courageous. If you are going to be a person of wisdom, you can't be of two minds. If you are going to pray don't worry. I want you to stop being dualistic in your thinking. Find the points in your life that you are struggling with and ask yourself if you are sending out two messages? Are you saying you want success, but sabotaging yourself when success comes? Are you saying you want money, but you don't want to put in the work to get it? Are you saying you want love, but you don't want to be around loving people? What is it that you are saying to yourself that blocks the very thing you say you want? You must let go of one of your thoughts. You must focus only on one path at a time. Be firm in a decision. Better to make a decision and have it be wrong, then to make no decision at all. You can always learn from mistakes, but never being able to decide keeps you in stagnation.

Questions:

1.   **What is your one goal for today?**

_____

_____

_____

2.   **What messages align with that goal?**

_____

_____

_____

3.   **What will you say to the thoughts that distract you from that goal?**

_____

_____

DAY 46 – GETTING UP FROM FAILURE

"Success is falling nine times and getting up ten."
– Jon Bon Jovi –

The greatest success in your life comes after you have had the greatest stumble. Keep trying. Keep moving forward. Shift your focus from the stumble to how you can use the experience and turn it into a success. There is no true failing - only a series of learning lessons or tools to help guide you along your way. Get up. Today, you might not feel like it. That's ok. Your feelings are valid. But, what are you going to do? Your feeling will change as you dust yourself off and try again.

There is nothing in your life that you can't learn and grow from. There is no mistake that is too big or mess that is too ugly that you can't clean it up. Don't try to erase the stumble. Don't try to go back in time and redo the past. I know this is tempting, but let the past be in the past. Tell yourself you won't do that again and move on. You will find yourself becoming all that you want to be, and you will look back on your stumbles as the very things that caused you to perfect your stride.

Questions:
1.   **What does "getting up" look like for you today?**

_____

_____

_____

2.   **How will you motivate yourself throughout the day?**

_____

_____

_____

JOURNAL:

_____

_____

_____

DAY 47 – THE PAST HAS NO POWER

"The past has no power over the present moment."
– Eckhart Tolle –

Learn to let things go. In this moment you have power. Your past is not holding you captive. Your past is not holding you back. As you learn to live in the present and really own who you are, you regain the power you seemingly lost. You can do it. Be present. Be in the now. Be powerful today.

Questions:

1.   What do you see around you?

_____

_____

_____

2.   What do you smell?

_____

_____

_____

3.   What do you see?

_____

_____

_____

JOURNAL:

_____

_____

_____

_____

_____

_____

DAY 48 – FINDING YOUR AIM

"Our plans miscarry because they have no aim. When a man does not know what harbor he is making for, no wind is the right wind."
– Seneca –

Do you know where you are going today? What do you want to get out of the conversation you are starting with your coworker or family member? Have you thought about it? What is it that you want from this experience right now? Are you just letting life happen to you or are you pointing yourself to where you want to go? There is nothing that can help you, if you cannot first help or direct yourself. Just the very thought of where you want to go brings the "wind" that you need.

You need to set your intentions before you begin each moment of this day. Be determined today to aim for the harbor you want. Don't drift. Helpful winds will come and assist you once your boat is pointed to your harbor.

Questions:
1. **What is it that you want?**

_____

_____

_____

2. **How will you get what you want?**

_____

_____

_____

JOURNAL:

_____

_____

_____

_____

DAY 49 – LIFE IS LIKE A JEWEL MINE

"Life without endeavor is like entering a jewel mine and coming out with empty hands."

– Japanese Proverb –

What are you striving for today? Wondering around life, without an endeavor and an intent to get the very best for yourself, is like going into a jewel mine and coming out empty handed. That's just crazy! Take a moment and look around you. Find the jewels. Don't rush around in such a state that you pass over the very things you are looking for. You will find there are jewels all around you. You are truly wealthy.

Questions:

1. **How will you slow down today?**

_____

_____

_____

2. **What jewels are sitting right in front of you?**

_____

_____

JOURNAL:

_____

_____

_____

_____

_____

_____

_____

_____

DAY 50 – HAPPY IS A BY-PRODUCT

"Happiness is not a goal, but a by-product."
– Eleanor Roosevelt –

Happiness is not your goal. Happiness comes from you being You. Only you can be You. Your goal is to be all that you can be. Your goal is to uncover and develop yourself in whatever direction you want to take. There are no limits. There is no end. And along the way, the by-product of you being yourself will be happiness. So, go be you today.

Questions:

1.   **What makes you unique?**

_____

_____

_____

2.   **How are you going to develop or use your special qualities today?**

_____

_____

JOURNAL: _____

_____

_____

_____

_____

_____

_____

_____

_____

_____

"Don't bunt. Aim out of the ballpark."
– David Obilvy –

Are you really in the game of life? Are you putting your all into everything you do, or are you taking cheap shots? You are better than that. Come on. Get your head in the game and aim out of the ballpark. When you try your best you may find you hit a few homeruns now and again. I know you can do it!

Questions:

1.　**What are you aiming for?**

_____

_____

_____

2.　**Are you trying your best?**

_____

_____

_____

3.　**What two areas can you do better in?**

_____

_____

JOURNAL:

_____

_____

_____

_____

_____

DAY 52 – GIVE SOMETHING BACK

"Life is a gift, and it offers us the privilege, opportunity, and responsibility to give something back by becoming more."
– Tony Robbins –

Everything we experience in our life is a gift. Take the opportunity today to give back. Give back to yourself and to others. It is through the act of giving that we receive. We receive so that we can then again give. Allow this exchange to happen. Allow the flow of giving and receiving to nourish your life. You will find yourself strengthened and encouraged as you do.

Questions:

1. **What can you give to yourself today?**

_____

_____

_____

2. **What can you give to someone else today?**

_____

_____

_____

3. **What have you received today?**

_____

_____

_____

JOURNAL:

_____

_____

150 DAYS OF
PEACE

"Nature and wisdom never are at strife."
– Plutarch –

Wisdom is a lot like nature. When I think of nature, I often think of two things – order and balance. Wisdom calls us to operate in order and from a place of balance. Today, I want you to see what things need to be put in order. Ask yourself if you are balanced in the thoughts that you are thinking. Before long, you will find wisdom is flowing through you and to you.

Questions:

1. **What do you need to put in order?**

_____

_____

_____

2. **What balances you out?**

_____

_____

_____

JOURNAL:

_____

_____

_____

_____

_____

_____

_____

_____

_____

150 DAYS OF
PEACE

DAY 54 – YOU HAVE WHAT IT TAKES

"There are no classes in life for beginners: right away you are always asked to deal with what is most difficult."
– Rainer Maria Rike –

Life is not for beginners; it is for the advanced. You are advanced. You have what it takes. You might be facing challenges, but you have all the answers and everything you need to pass this test. Give yourself more credit. You are better than you think.

Questions:

1. **What is today's challenge?**

_____

_____

_____

2. **What answer do you already have to meet this challenge?**

_____

_____

_____

3. **How have things positively worked out for you in the past?**

_____

_____

_____

JOURNAL:

_____

_____

_____

_____

> **"We are responsible for what we are,
> and whatever we wish ourselves to be,
> we have the power to make ourselves."**
> **– Swami Vivekananda –**

The beauty about life is that you have the responsibility and the opportunity to change it. You are not held captive or victim to your situation. You are the victor in making everything you want come true. Today, I want you to take responsibility for both the positive and negative situations you have created. Don't run and hide. Stand up and do something for you. You are not waiting for others to bring the answers to you or do the work for you.

You are in control of your own choices. You can create a different outcome for yourself. This is both sobering and liberating. Life has given you a gift. Now go use it wisely.

Questions:

1.   **What do you need to take responsibility for?**

_____

_____

_____

2.   **What opportunity are you going to create for yourself?**

_____

_____

_____

JOURNAL: _____

_____

_____

_____

_____

DAY 56 – EDUCATION IN ADVERSITY

"There is no education like adversity."
– Benjamin Disraeli –

A little adversity; a little challenge; a little controversy; a little challenge is actually really good for us. Sometimes your adversity is your best teacher. Remember you want to learn and grow. Your adversity is causing just that. Adversity comes when you need to experience the situation to really understand the lesson it teaches. Embrace the lesson and the adversity will subside.

Questions:

1. **What adversity are you going through?**

_____

_____

_____

2. **What lesson is your adversity trying to teach you?**

_____

_____

_____

3. **How will you apply what you are learning today?**

_____

_____

_____

JOURNAL:

_____

_____

_____

_____

DAY 57 – FOCUS ON POSITIVITY

"How much pain have cost us the evils that have never happened."
– Thomas Jefferson –

Are you worried about something that hasn't happened? Are you anticipating a problem? You are the creator of your own experience. Focusing on pain and suffering will only bring you more pain and suffering. Either the event will happen because you forced it to happen or it will never happen and you have worried for nothing. Most of the negative things we think about are pointless. They do nothing to prepare us for life or move us forward to what we truly want. Be confident that you have everything you need for each moment.

Don't run out ahead of yourself and create conflict unnecessarily. Stay rooted in this moment and make the positive choices now and you will see tomorrow take care of itself. And you just might find that all those "evils" never really happened.

Questions:

1.   **Are you worrying? How is the worrying helping?**

_____

_____

_____

2.   **What action could you take to solve the problem?**

_____

_____

_____

3.   **What could you focus on instead of your problem?**

_____

_____

_____

DAY 58 – STAY SOFT

> "Be soft. Do not let the world make you hard.
> Do not let pain make you hate.
> Do not let the bitterness steal your sweetness.
> Take pride that even though the rest of the world may
> disagree, you still believe it to be a beautiful place."
> – Curt Vonnegut –

Are you going through something that has left you discouraged? Do you feel jaded? I want to encourage you that this hardship is making you stronger. What you are going through is here to bring you more clarity. Don't let pain or hardships make you bitter. Don't let discouragement strip you of your essence. If other's keep telling you that there is no hope, don't listen to them.

Look around and find your own version of beauty. Believe that voice inside yourself that says you can. What do YOU want? Who cares how old or young you are? Who cares what you have or have not been through? What does it matter if things were fair? Rest. Breath. Soften. You are beautiful and you live in a beautiful world.

Questions:
1.   **How are you beautiful?**

_____

_____

_____

2.   **What will you do to show your softer side?**

_____

_____

_____

JOURNAL:

_____

_____

DAY 59 – KEEP GOING

> ### "Some men give up their designs when they have almost reached the goal; while others, on the contrary, obtain a victory by exerting, at the last moment, more vigorous efforts than before."
> – Polybius –

If you quit, you will never know what could have been. Tired? Reach a little bit more. Slow? Pick up the pace. Unfocused? Put your mind to the task at hand. There will be a time to rest, to slow down, and to let your mind wander. Those are all necessary and balancing activities. But for now keep going. If you don't make your deadline – fine. You know better for next time. If you don't reach your goal – so be it. But you never know when that little bit of effort or that little extra push is all it takes to cross over your finish line. Be encouraged today. Get your second wind. Keep going. You can do it.

Questions:

1.   **How will you give extra effort today?**

_____

_____

_____

2.   **In what are you doing well?**

_____

_____

_____

3.   **What action will you do to go above and beyond expectations?**

_____

_____

_____

JOURNAL: _____

DAY 60 – PURPOSE GIVES MEANING

"Purpose is what give is life a meaning."
– C. H. Parkhurst –

Life is not meant to be experienced in autopilot. As you live a life of purpose, you direct the events of your life and those events move to your will. You are the one who gives meaning to life, not the other way around. Don't get hung up on what your big purpose in life is. Your true Self knows what you are doing and where you are going. Just know and believe that you are the one who is giving value and direction to everything around you. Move ahead with intent and decisiveness and life will reflect back the meaning you have been looking for.

Questions:

1.   **What do you purpose today?**

_____

_____

_____

2.   **What area of life are you taking off autopilot?**

_____

_____

JOURNAL:

_____

_____

_____

_____

_____

_____

_____

_____

DAY 61 – HAPPINESS IS A CHOICE

"Happiness, like unhappiness, is a proactive choice."
– Stephen Covey –

It takes as much work to be happy as it does to be unhappy. Today, when you are faced with any situation, make the choice that lifts you up. You know what I am talking about. Take the high road. Be your better Self. You are going to put energy toward the situation anyway. Why not put a positive spin on it? Why not look at the benefits of the situation? What you focus on brings more of the same. Be conscious in your thoughts and choose what lifts your spirit. You will find that you have a smile on your face and a spring in your step.

Questions:

1.	**What is good about this moment?**

_____

_____

_____

2.	**What three positive actions will you take in the next three hours?**

_____

_____

_____

JOURNAL: _____

_____

_____

_____

_____

_____

_____

_____

150 DAYS OF PEACE

"Life is either a daring adventure or nothing."
– Helen Keller –

Today is your day to be daring. Strive for the best. Throw caution to the wind. Give it all you have. Stop being timid. Go on an adventure. Do something that is a bit outside your comfort zone. Talk to a stranger or sign up for a new class. Take dancing lessons or try a new food. Create your own dare and then take yourself up on it. The point is, just do it. Besides having fun, you will find yourself living a life that is daring and dynamic.

Questions:

1.   **What do you dare yourself to do?**

_____

_____

_____

2.   **What action right now will you do to put this dare into action?**

_____

_____

_____

JOURNAL:

_____

_____

_____

_____

_____

_____

_____

_____

_____

DAY 63 – CALAMITY IS A VALUABLE HINT

"Every calamity is a spur and a valuable hint."
– Ralph Waldo Emerson –

Life gives us little hints. You are getting clues as to where you are now and what is ahead of you. What you are experiencing is in fact some sort of pattern. Pay attention today to the little moments. See the clues that are being revealed to you. Nothing is a coincidence. The world is unfolding around you to help you along your path. Suggestions are being given to you as to which way is most beneficial to you. Training yourself to be aware of these hints will move you more quickly in the direction you want to go.

Questions:

1.   **What is the universe saying to you?**

_____

_____

_____

2.   **How might these messages help direct your path today?**

_____

_____

_____

JOURNAL:

_____

_____

_____

_____

_____

_____

_____

_____

DAY 64 – SEIZE THE MOMENT

"When one door of happiness closes, another opens, but often we look so long at the closed door that we do not see the one that has been opened for us."
– Helen Keller –

Are you living with regret? Doors open all the time for you. If you are focused on the opportunity that didn't happen, or if you are regretting all the things that "weren't", then you will never see the new opportunity that replaced the lost opportunity. You cannot move smoothly forward when you are looking back over your shoulder. It is ok! Let go of what you have been holding on to. Something new is happening. There is a door that is wide open, and you just need to step through it. A door just closed? No worries. Keep your eyes opened for the next door that will open for you.

Questions:

1.   **What door is open right now in your life?**

_____

_____

_____

2.   **What are three actions that will allow you to walk through this open door?**

_____

_____

JOURNAL:

_____

_____

_____

_____

_____

150 DAYS OF
PEACE

DAY 65 – YOUR COMFORT ZONE

"If we're growing, we're always going to be out of our comfort zone."
– John C. Maxwell –

I want to encourage you that if you are going through an uncomfortable situation it means you are growing. You are not being punished for something you did. You are in fact starting to move forward in new areas that previously were unfamiliar to you. Just remind yourself that all of your experiences, in this area, are new and that in time you will adjust. Be encouraged to continue practicing and learning. In time you will master all that is now uncomfortable. Good job! Keep up the good work.

Questions:

1.   **What is new for you today?**

_____

_____

_____

2.   **How are you going to get more comfortable with this new situation?**

_____

_____

_____

3.   **What will you tell yourself when you feel like avoiding your new area of growth?**

_____

_____

_____

JOURNAL:

_____

_____

_____

DAY 66 – GO LIVE LIFE

"The best way to prepare for life is to begin to live."
– Elbert Hubard –

Life doesn't come with a manual or a set of instructions for everything you do. The best way to prepare for life is to simply live. Live in the moment. Live in the challenges. Live in the successes. Live in the good, and live in the bad. Then, and only then, will you find yourself growing and prepared for whatever comes your way. There is no way around it. So today – just go live life.

Questions:

1.   What have you put on hold because you don't feel you have the answer?

_____

_____

_____

2.   How might you be able to answer your own questions about this situation?

_____

_____

_____

3.   What action will you do today to live in and through this situation?

_____

_____

_____

JOURNAL:

_____

_____

_____

_____

150 DAYS OF
PEACE

"All sunshine makes the desert."
– Arabian Proverb –

Do you want sunshine all the time? What if you got your wish and you only had sun? No rain, no clouds, just hot blistering sun? Well, then you would indeed be asking for something other than sun. So too is your life. Be thankful for every season. We need sun and rain and everything in-between. Only then will you have a healthy and thriving environment.

Questions:

1.   **What season is your life in?**

_____

_____

_____

2.   **How can you be thankful for this period in your life?**

_____

_____

_____

3.   **What lessons can you take with you as this season comes to an end?**

_____

_____

_____

JOURNAL:

_____

_____

_____

_____

150 DAYS OF PEACE

"The purpose of life is a life of purpose."
– Robert Byrne –

Have you asked yourself the question, "Why am I here?" Instead of looking for the big picture and waiting for the answer, look for the small answers that you already have, and the big picture will unfold for you. Make the "little" things throughout your day meaningful and full of purpose. Don't float along waiting for something to happen to you. Find the joy and the life in everything you do today. Continue doing this and you will see that your life will start taking on purpose and direction.

Questions:

1.   **What are six things small activities that you will purpose to do?**

_____

_____

_____

2.   **How will you find joy in those actions?**

_____

_____

_____

JOURNAL:

_____

_____

_____

_____

_____

_____

_____

_____

_____

150 DAYS OF
PEACE

"Everyone here has the sense that right now is one of those moments when we are influencing the future."
– Steve Jobs –

It is such a powerful experience to be right now in this moment. Do you know that in this moment you are doing things and being someone that will impact your tomorrow? You are thinking things that are not only changing your world but are actually changing the future. I want you to realize that today. You are powerful. Even though you can't see it right now—the decisions you are making, and the way that you are thinking is going to change your life so dramatically. You will look back and one day tell yourself, "THIS was the moment—right here right now—that I changed my future."

Questions:

1.   **How will you appreciate this moment?**

_____

_____

_____

2.   **How does this moment make you excited about your future?**

_____

_____

_____

JOURNAL: _____

_____

_____

_____

_____

_____

_____

DAY 70 – LOVE MORE AND MORE

"As I grow to understand life less and less, I learn to love it more and more."
– Jules Renard –

Have you been working hard? Have you been studying and learning? I know you have. And yet there is always more to learn and more to experience. There is a joy to learning. You never want to stop. And there is always a moment where you understand how little you really do understand. You are perfect right where you are. Love all that you have been becoming. Enjoy the world around you. Let the love in you flow out from you. And, keep up the good work.

Questions:

1. **What have you learned this past week?**

_____

_____

_____

2. **What do you want to learn more of?**

_____

_____

JOURNAL:

_____

_____

_____

_____

_____

_____

_____

150 DAYS OF
PEACE

"To change one's life: Start immediately. Do it flamboyantly. NO exceptions."
– William James –

Whatever your intention or goal is, don't hesitate. Do it right away. What are you waiting for? What is holding you back? Now throw all of those excuses away and get to work. There is nothing holding you back. Only you can stop you. Jump right in and start living your dream. You are worth it and you can do it.

Questions:

1.   **What is one goal you have stopped pursuing?**

_____

_____

_____

2.   **What will you do today to move you closer to that goal?**

_____

_____

_____

JOURNAL:

_____

_____

_____

_____

_____

_____

_____

_____

DAY 72 – LETTING GO

"Learn to hold loosely all that is not eternal."
– A. Maude Royden –

What are you giving value to? What is worth most to you? Today, I want you to place your value in what will last. You are eternal. You are therefore very valuable. Anything you do for yourself to nurture and develop you is worthwhile. Find other areas in your life that are lasting. Place your time and energy into those things too. Let go of everything else.

Don't hang on to the trivial problems or situations that do not serve you. You are better than that, and you have more important things to do and take care of. So today, loosen your grip on things that aren't that important, and focus on what truly matters and what is eternal.

Questions:
1.   **What is valuable to you today?**

_____

_____

_____

2.   **How are you going to cherish and grow what is valuable?**

_____

_____

_____

JOURNAL:

_____

_____

_____

_____

_____

DAY 73 – HATE NEVER SOLVED PROBLEMS

"Hate. It has caused a lot of problems in this world but has not solved one yet."
– Maya Angelou –

Hate has never solved any problems. Today, make it simple. Go out and love. Be a part of the solution. This is all you need to do today is find ways to be love and show love.

Questions:

1.   **How will you receive love?**

_____

_____

_____

2.   **How will you give love?**

_____

_____

JOURNAL: _____

_____

_____

_____

_____

_____

_____

_____

_____

DAY 74 – GOING IS THE GOAL

"The going is the goal."
– Horace Kallen –

Get going! You have planned enough and thought about it enough. You know what you want and you even know how you are going to get it. So go! Today, the goal is to keep going and going and going. If nothing else, don't stop. You will be able to look back at the end of the day and say, "WOW, look at all I did." Now go do it!

Questions:

1. **Why are you still here?**

_____

_____

_____

2. **What are you going to go do?**

_____

_____

JOURNAL:

_____

_____

_____

_____

_____

_____

_____

_____

_____

_____

DAY 75 – LOVE LIFE

"To live is like to love—all reason is against it, and all healthy instinct for it."
– Samuel Butler –

When you are in love, you do crazy things. And, you do those crazy things all out of instinct. Anyone looking from the outside might say that what you are doing doesn't make sense, and you aren't being reasonable. Today, I want you to go with your gut feeling. I want you to trust your instincts. Don't worry about what others say of you or think of you. You are crazy. Own it. Your crazy idea today will be the brilliant idea of tomorrow. So, go be crazy!

Questions:

1.   **What larger-than-life idea do you have?**

_____

_____

_____

2.   **How can you have fun with this idea today?**

_____

_____

JOURNAL:

_____

_____

_____

_____

_____

_____

_____

_____

_____

150 DAYS OF
PEACE

DAY 76 – TAKE SMALL STEPS

"Put your heart, mind, and soul into even your smallest acts. This is the secret of success."
– Swami Sivaananda –

Are you in a rush to get to your goal? Reaching your goal takes a lot of small steps. You know this. So, you might say there is no such thing as a small act, because it is from those "small acts" that the larger picture of success is achieved. Be at peace today with whatever you have to do. Love the little things, and keep moving forward.

Questions:
1.   **What are ten 'little" things you have to do today?**

_____

_____

_____

2.   **How will you celebrate the completion of those ten things?**

_____

_____

_____

JOURNAL:

_____

_____

_____

_____

_____

_____

_____

_____

DAY 77 – FRACTURES MAKE US STRONG

"Fractures well cured make us more strong."
– Ralph Waldo Emerson –

Are you feeling broken? Is there any area of your life that seems fractured? If so, make sure you take the time to heal. Don't worry. Work will be waiting for you when you get back. Take a vacation. Rest. Let someone else take care of you. Release any guilt you have because of where you find yourself. You need to heal. And take comfort in the fact that after you heal (and you will) you will be stronger. The very broken and fractured areas will be the strongest. So today, if you need to take some time off, go do it. Relax and repair. Go get some sleep.

Questions:

1.   **What do you need to repair?**

_____

_____

_____

2.   **How are you going to heal yourself today?**

_____

_____

JOURNAL:

_____

_____

_____

_____

_____

_____

_____

_____

DAY 78 – BE AROUND GREATNESS

"Great people, no matter their field, have similar habits. Learn them and use them in your own quest for greatness."
– Paula Andress –

Surround yourself with people who cause greatness to come from you. You might feel a little uncomfortable at first. Maybe you feel you are not as knowledgeable or experienced as these people. Good! Listen to them. Understand how they work. Learn, learn, learn. You will find yourself growing in areas that you never knew possible.

Questions:

1.   **Who do you admire?**

_____

_____

_____

2.   **What good habits can you learn from them?**

_____

_____

_____

3.   **Where can you find people who inspire you?**

_____

_____

_____

4.   **How will you connect with them on a regular basis?**

_____

_____

_____

DAY 79 – STAND IN YOUR OWN SUNSHINE

"Most of the shadows of this life are caused by our standing in our own sunshine."
– Ralph Waldo Emerson –

Are you casting a shadow over your own life? Are you blocking yourself? You are wonderful and powerful and when you decide to be anything else, you cast hindrances onto your own path. No one is doing this to you. There is not a problem you face that is out of your control or that is happening to you. You are the master and creator of your own choices. And, there IS a light that is within you. Let your light out. Let yourself shine. Quit casting shadows over your dreams. Enjoy who you are and let the world see your light.

Questions:
1.   **What shadows are you standing in?**

_____

_____

_____

2.   **What action will you take to step into your own light?**

_____

_____

_____

JOURNAL: _____

_____

_____

_____

_____

_____

_____

150 DAYS OF
PEACE

"If you don't know where you are going, you'll end up someplace else."
– Yogi Berra –

The "someplace else" in your life is the unknown or the situation you didn't plan on getting into. These can be very scary places. You find yourself in these places because you didn't know where you were going in the first place. You need to be very clear where you want to go before you set out on your journey. Ask yourself what you intend. What do want? What is the purpose of this activity? What do I want to get out of this experience?

Questions:

1.   **Where are you going?**

_____

_____

_____

2.   **Where are you now?**

_____

_____

_____

3.   **What actions today most align with where you want to be?**

_____

_____

JOURNAL:

_____

_____

_____

DAY 81 – OBSTACLES ARE INCENTIVES

"Obstacles are great incentives."
– Jules Michelet –

Obstacles are neither good nor bad. It is your perspective that you put on obstacles that really determines the difference. Your perspective will influence the outcome of any obstacles you face today. You can either have an obstacle crisis, or an obstacle course.

Are you seeing your obstacles as overcoming you or something to be overcome? I want you to shift your focus and even make it a game. Make it an obstacle course and intend to master each hurdle. How fast can you jump or how low can you crawl? Test your agility and endurance. And, at the end of the course look back and say, "Yes! I did that."

Questions:
1.   **What is your obstacle today?**

_____

_____

_____

2.   **How will you turn an obstacle crisis into an obstacle course?**

_____

_____

_____

JOURNAL:

_____

_____

_____

_____

_____

150 DAYS OF
PEACE

"Whatever you want to do, do it now.
There are only so many tomorrows."
– Michael Landon –

What are you waiting for? You have the tools. You have the knowledge. You have the support that you need. Tomorrow is never going to be here. Now is your opportunity. Now is your time. This is what you were meant to do. You don't need any more permission. Do it NOW!

Questions:

1.   **What activity have you been putting off?**

_____

_____

_____

2.   **What action will you do today to finish what you started?**

_____

_____

_____

3.   **How will you hold yourself accountable?**

_____

_____

_____

JOURNAL:

_____

_____

_____

_____

150 DAYS OF PEACE

"Nothing is impossible, the word itself says 'I'm possible'."
– Audrey Hepburn –

Are you giving possibility to things going wrong? Are you giving possibility to others but not yourself? Look inside of yourself and tell yourself that you are possible. Don't let anything get you down today. Tell yourself that you can do it and that everything is possible.

Questions:

1.   What have you told yourself is impossible.

_____

_____

_____

2.   What are you going to do to change your perspective?

_____

_____

_____

3.   How are you going to take your new perspective and turn it into action?

_____

_____

_____

JOURNAL:

_____

_____

_____

_____

DAY 84 – LIFE IS AN OPPORTUNITY

"We become happier, much happier, when we realize life is an opportunity rather than an obligation."
– Mary Augustine –

I am sure you don't like to feel obligated to do anything. I know I don't. Has life and your daily activities become a bit of an obligation for you? Do you dread your work or family life? Maybe you committed yourself to something, and now it seems more of a chore than a joy. This can easily happen. And while you might not be able to get out of all of those obligations you signed up for, you can change your perspective about them.

Today, I want you to tell yourself that each of these obligations are a gift. Tell yourself that they are an opportunity for you to practice being your better Self. Set an intent of what you want to learn in each situation, and go face the day with a new outlook. I guarantee it will help.

Questions:
1.   **What obligation would you rather not do?**

_____

_____

_____

2.   **How can you look at this situation in a positive light?**

_____

_____

_____

3.   **What can you glean from this experience?**

_____

_____

_____

DAY 85 – FEAR KILLS DREAMS

"There is only one thing that makes a dream impossible to achieve: the fear of failure."
– Paulo Coelho –

Your dream is only impossible if you tell yourself it is. What is it about achieving your goal that you fear the most? Some idea is holding you back. And, your fear probably seems very real to you. Please understand that all fear is trying to do is keep you safe. Are you safe? Are your fears founded, or do you really know deep down inside that your fear has no basis? Sure, moving out into new territory is scary.

There is a reason people stay in the comfort zone—it is comfortable. But, if you can look at your fear and understand that you are indeed safe and that your fear is unfounded, then you can begin to move past your fear. And, once you have moved past your fear, nothing is impossible for you.

Questions:
1.   **What are you afraid of?**

_____

_____

_____

2.   **Is your fear rational?**

_____

_____

_____

3.   **What are you going to do today to move past your fear?**

_____

_____

_____

JOURNAL:

DAY 86 – GOALS WITHIN SIGHT

"Your goal should be just out of reach, but not out of sight."
– Denis Waitley & Remi Witt –

If you have a goal or vision that is out of sight it might not be your goal or your dream. So, if your dream doesn't seem like it is in the scope of what you can accomplish, ask yourself if it is really yours. When you have a vision or goal that is truly yours, your dream will always be in sight.

Yes, you might feel like it is a bit out of your reach, but you can see it, and move forward to it. So today, if you feel like something is out of sight, check in with yourself to see if you are following your dream or someone else's.

Questions:
1.   **Is your goal really yours?**

_____

_____

_____

2.   **What would you do if you didn't have to please anyone?**

_____

_____

_____

3.   **What are you doing today to propel you forward to your own dream?**

_____

_____

_____

JOURNAL:

_____

_____

DAY 87 – ABILITIES ARE SHOWN THROUGH ADVERSITY

"Success in the affairs of life often serves to hide one's abilities, whereas adversity frequently gives on an opportunity to discover them."
– Horace –

I do want you to celebrate your successes. You have earned that right. Go have fun. Congratulations! Ok, now what? What is next? I want you to learn to keep growing and moving forward during the good times. Don't wait until hardship comes to show your real abilities.

I know it might be easier to step up to a challenge and be all that you can be in the moment of adversity. But, do you really need adversity to show your abilities? And, if you do find yourself in adversity, then celebrate the opportunity to use all of your talents to come up with a brilliant solution. Either way, keep growing and moving forward to your goal.

Questions:
1.   **What are your abilities?**

_____

_____

_____

2.   **How are you using them today?**

_____

_____

JOURNAL: _____

_____

_____

_____

DAY 88 – WE'RE ALL CONNECTED

"I do believe we're all connected. I do believe in positive energy. I do believe in the power of prayer. I do believe in putting good out into the world. And I believe in taking care of each other."
– Harvey Fierstein –

You have belief in something or someone. I want you to believe and know today that everything is working out for your good. Have belief that people are good. Have belief in yourself. We are all connected and we are collectively making this world a better place. Go do your part today. I know you can.

Questions:

1.   **What or who do you believe in?**

_____

_____

_____

2.   **How are you going to put good out into the world today?**

_____

_____

_____

JOURNAL:

_____

_____

_____

_____

_____

_____

DAY 89 – LIFE IS ACTIVE WORK

"Life, in all ranks and situations, is an outward occupation, an actual and active work."
– W. Humboldt –

Your job is not your real job. What do I mean? Whatever you do for an occupation is not the main work you are here to do. What you are doing right now is your real work. Yes, reading this is your work. Living life is your work. Every moment of each day is what you are really here to do. And all of those little moments add up to your great purpose. Give as much attention to living life as you do your nine-to-five job. You will find that life is more rewarding.

Questions:

1.   **What do you want to be known for?**

_____

_____

_____

2.   **How are you acting in this moment?**

_____

_____

_____

3.   **Does your overall goal and this moment line up?**

_____

_____

_____

JOURNAL:

_____

_____

_____

_____

DAY 90 – HAPPY TRAVELING

"Happiness is not a state to arrive at, but a manner of traveling."
– Margaret Lee Runbeck –

Think of happiness like a road trip. Think of going to your favorite destination. You have been anticipating this trip for a long time. Now you are on your trip and your travel companions are fighting. Before long you are fighting with them. Then the traffic slows and your car stops. Three hours later you finally get through the traffic jam. You are upset and grumpy. You are hungry and tired. Sound miserable doesn't it?

Don't spend energy planning for a wonderful destination, all while hating the trip to your destination. Enjoy each step of your trip. Finding your happiness in every moment allows you to travel life with enjoyment.

Questions:
1.   **What are you plans for today?**

_____

_____

_____

2.   **How are you going to enjoy the unfolding of those plans?**

_____

_____

_____

JOURNAL:

_____

_____

_____

_____

_____

_____

DAY 91 – TAKE CHANGES

"Take chances, make mistakes. That's how you grow. Pain nourishes your courage. You have to fail in order to practice being brave."
– Mary Tyler Moore –

Growth take bravery. Bravery takes practice. Life is a practice. You make mistakes. That's ok. Today keep practicing. Keep going. You can do it.

Questions:

1. **What are you practicing today?**

_____

_____

_____

2. **What action will you try to improve?**

_____

_____

_____

JOURNAL:

_____

_____

_____

_____

_____

_____

_____

_____

_____

_____

_____

DAY 92 – ADVERSITY IS THE MOTHER OF PROGRESS

"Adversity is the mother of progress."
– Mahatma Gandhi –

Most of us don't look at adversity as being a good thing. But, the adversity in your life today is giving birth to the progress you are going to experience now and in the future. Take some time to reflect on how far you have come and how much growth you already have experienced.

Be at peace with where you know you currently are on your path. Be at peace towards the goals you have set. You are doing a great job. Smile at any adversity you experience today. You know you are making progress.

Questions:
1.   **What area in your life has seen the most progress?**

_____

_____

_____

2.   **What will you say to yourself if you encounter adversity today?**

_____

_____

JOURNAL:
_____

_____

_____

_____

_____

_____

_____

150 DAYS OF
PEACE

DAY 93 – OVERLOOK SMALL THINGS

"The art of being wise is knowing what to overlook."
– William James –

Wisdom does not get bogged down with details that would cause imbalance. Often we let little situations or discomforts direct and dictate our mood and feelings. Today, I want you to challenge yourself to let go of the little stuff. Let go of the people who don't behave the way you want them to or the situation that didn't quite go as planned.

Ask yourself if it is worth getting worked-up over. The answer is always no. So, take a moment to center yourself and reaffirm that everything is working out just the way it should. Tell yourself that you are safe and can handle any situation that comes across your path. Now, go have a great day.

Questions:

1. **What three situations can you let go of?**

_____

_____

_____

2. **What positive idea will you focus on today?**

_____

_____

JOURNAL:

_____

_____

_____

_____

_____

_____

_____

150 DAYS OF
PEACE

"We accept the love that we think we deserve."
– Stephen Chbosky –

Do you feel you deserve love? This is a great question. You might be blocking love because you think that you haven't earned it. Love is all around you. Love comes in many different forms and from many sources. I am here to tell you that you deserve love. This is true. I do not care what you have done in your past or what people have said about you.

You are love and you deserve love. Love is right in front of you and more of it is on its way. Today, I want you to open up your heart just a little bit more and let some of that love in.

Questions:

1.   **How can you see love right now?**

_____

_____

_____

2.   **Are you open to this love?**

_____

_____

_____

3.   **What are some ways you might be blocking love?**

_____

_____

_____

4.   **What action are you going to take today to open yourself up to love?**

_____

_____

150 DAYS OF
PEACE

DAY 95 – CONSIDER THE END

"In all things that you do, consider the end."
– Solon –

Do you start a project and then fail to follow through? Do you have conversations with people and find yourself saying or doing things you regret later? It has happened to all of us. When you find yourself 'stuck' it most likely is because you didn't think about what you wanted to achieve from the project or situation. Today, I want you to take a moment to think before you do. Think before you say. This is one of those old principles that has stood the test of time. Ask yourself, "What do I want?"

As you are more thoughtful and intentful today, you will see the results you have been looking for. And, for those projects that have been unfinished, maybe you need to wrap them up or maybe you just need to let them go. Either way, allow yourself the time to think before you say or do.

Questions:

1.   What do you need to finish?

_____

_____

_____

2.   What do you need to let go?

_____

_____

_____

3.   What are three questions you will ask yourself before you start anything new?

_____

_____

_____

JOURNAL:

DAY 96 – DO NOT WORRY ABOUT TOMORROW

"Therefore do not worry about tomorrow, for tomorrow will worry about itself. Each day has enough trouble of its own."
– Matthew 6:34 –

I also want to add—don't worry about yesterday. Worry will get you nowhere. Focusing on the past or the future stops you in the present. Today, you will focus on each moment. When you find your mind wandering—bring yourself back to the here-and-now.

You have everything it takes for right now in this moment. You will have everything you need for the next moment too. Trust and believe that you are capable, and that all things are working out for your good.

Questions:

1.   **What are you doing right now?**

_____

_____

_____

2.   **What is going well for you?**

_____

_____

_____

3.   **How have you shown yourself that you are capable?**

_____

_____

_____

JOURNAL:

_____

_____

DAY 97 – JUST MOVE ON

"You must make a decision that you are going to move on. It won't happen automatically. You will have to rise up and say. "I don't care how hard this is, I don't care how disappointed I am, I'm not going to let this get the best of me. I'm moving on with my life."
– Joel Osteen –

Yes, you have had those moments that have set you back or stalled you. But right now you are going to take life off of autopilot. Actively make a choice to press play. You are the only one who can do this. You will have to practice.

You might have to keep reminding yourself of how you are moving forward, but you can! Rise up and embrace this day. You have a wonderful life ahead of you.

Questions:

1. How will you move on today?

_____

_____

_____

2. How will you let go of your past?

_____

_____

_____

JOURNAL:

_____

_____

_____

_____

_____

DAY 98 – MISFORTUNE IS A STEPPING STONE TO FORTUNE

"All misfortune is but a stepping stone to fortune."
– Henry David Thoreau –

Misfortune clarifies what you want and where you are going. Misfortune also highlights areas we know we need to work on but for some reason haven't taken the time to address them.

All of your "troubles" are working to help you become a better version of yourself. Take the lesson to heart and move on your way to your personal fortune.

Questions:

1. **What situation or area in your life needs work?**

_____

_____

_____

2. **What are four actions today that you are going to do to clean it up?**

_____

_____

_____

JOURNAL:

_____

_____

_____

_____

_____

_____

_____

_____

DAY 99 – A GOAL IS A DREAM WITH A DEADLINE

"A goal is a dream with a deadline."
– Napoleon Hill –

You have dreams. However, dreams can be abstract. Goals give feet to your dreams and help make your dreams concrete. Your goals are helping you manifest these dreams. So, go be a dreamer but also be a goal-setter. Take the action required to live happily-ever-after.

Questions:

1.   **What is your dream today?**

_____

_____

_____

2.   **What are six actions you will take to make your dream come true?**

_____

_____

JOURNAL: _____

_____

_____

_____

_____

_____

_____

_____

_____

_____

150 DAYS OF
PEACE

"When I do good, I feel good. When I do bad, I feel bad. That's my religion."
– Abraham Lincoln –

Life is really simple. When we participate in "bad" actions we feel down. When we choose "good" actions, we feel much more like ourselves. You know this to be true. So, if you want to feel good today, simply do the actions that are going to give you positive results.

This day is in your hands and in your control. You have so many different options in front of you. Pick those activities, conversations, and actions that bring you joy and happiness. Make it simple.

Questions:
1. **What makes you happy?**

_____

_____

_____

2. **What action will you take in the next hour that will bring you positive results?**

_____

_____

_____

JOURNAL:

_____

_____

_____

_____

_____

_____

"Life's a voyage that's homeward bound."
– Herman Melville –

Home truly is where your heart or your desires are. Your wants and dreams are directing you to your "home"—the place where you feel like your true and better Self. So this brings us to the question, "Where is your heart?" Once you can answer that question, you can count on everything directing you to what you want.

There is no wrong answer and there is not a wrong path. You are here for a wonderful purpose and you are on a wonderful voyage.

Questions:

1.   Where is your heart today?

_____

_____

_____

2.   What actions line up with those feelings?

_____

_____

JOURNAL:

_____

_____

_____

_____

_____

_____

_____

DAY 102 – GREAT MINDS RISE ABOVE

"Little minds are tamed and subdued by misfortune, but great minds rise above them."
– Washington Irving –

You are not going to be tamed by your misfortune. You are strong and will rise above anything that comes your way. Remind yourself of this. If you see yourself today getting bogged down in the worries or fears of the moment than stop yourself and say, "I am not little minded!"

I know you want to be free to live your life and fulfill your dreams. So be free. Only you can put the chains around yourself. Only you can allow outside forces to tame you. You are doing a great job. Keep going. Have a wildly focused day.

Questions:

1.   **How will you loosen a chain that you have placed on yourself?**

_____

_____

_____

2.   **How will you rise above a fear today?**

_____

_____

_____

JOURNAL:

_____

_____

_____

_____

_____

_____

150 DAYS OF
PEACE

"The best way to gain self-confidence is to do what you are afraid to do."
– Unknown –

What are you afraid to do? What are you afraid to be? Self-confidence comes by practicing overcoming little fears. Eventually you will have enough courage to face a bigger fear and so on. You grow in confidence each time you allow yourself to go through something you are unsure of. Being uncomfortable is not always a bad thing.

So today, if you feel shy or timid or fearful, practice actions that prove to yourself that you can be a bit bolder than you thought. And if you don't do so well, try again. Eventually you will find your voice and stand on your own two feet with your head held high.

Questions:

1.   **What are you afraid of today?**

_____

_____

_____

2.   **What is one small step that you can practice today to conquer this fear?**

_____

_____

_____

JOURNAL:

_____

_____

_____

_____

_____

_____

DAY 104 – REACH: GO BEYOND YOURSELF

"Ah, but a man's reach should exceed his grasp, or what's a heaven for?"
– Robert Browning –

You need to go a little bit beyond yourself. This causes you to push yourself and grow. If your goal is just a little higher than you feel comfortable, and if you occasionally fall a little short of your goal, that's ok. Get back up and try again. This forward-reaching causes you to get a little stronger, a little bolder, and a little wiser each time. You are moving yourself in the direction you want.

Today, make sure you are setting goals that ask a little bit more of you. And, if you don't get everything done don't worry. Try again tomorrow.

Questions:
1.   **How can you push yourself today?**

_____

_____

_____

2.   **What are three actions you want to do in the next three hours?**

_____

_____

_____

JOURNAL:

_____

_____

_____

_____

_____

_____

DAY 105 – CHOOSE HAPPINESS

"Happiness is an attitude. We either make ourselves miserable or happy and strong. The amount of work is the same."

– Francesca Reigler –

You are going to work today. There is no way out of it. So, why not choose to be happy? You don't have to miserable. There is nothing that has to change in your life before you can choose to be happy. You are in control of your perspective. You are the one doing the work. You can say "no" or "yes" to a thought or an action.

There is nothing controlling you. Only you can do the work, and only you can choose which kind of work you want to do. Today, do the work of happiness. You will be glad you did.

Questions:

1.   **How are you going to be happy today?**

_____

_____

_____

2.   **What are two things you are happy about in this moment?**

_____

_____

JOURNAL:

_____

_____

_____

_____

_____

150 DAYS OF PEACE

DAY 106 – LIFE IS IN THE MOMENTS

"Life isn't a matter of milestones, but of moments."
– Rose Kennedy –

Are you living your life waiting for the milestones or the "big thing" to happen? Focus today on the little moments. Enjoy each one. The little moments are creating the milestone moments. You won't miss anything and you will find yourself getting to the "big" moments sooner. Maximize this moment and then plan on doing the same for each moment after.

Questions:

1.   **How are you going to maximize this moment now?**

_____

_____

_____

2.   **What will help remind you to stay in each moment?**

_____

_____

JOURNAL:

_____

_____

_____

_____

_____

_____

_____

_____

_____

DAY 107 – DO NOT QUIT

"The difference in winning and losing is most often...not quitting."
– Walt Disney –

Have you ever wondered what made the difference in a person who wins and a person who loses? Most of the time it is a choice to not quit. No one said it was easy. No one promised that there wouldn't be hard work. But you know that you can win at this game of life. And by winning, I mean reach the goals and the place where you feel you want to be.

Don't compare yourself to others. Don't worry about what anyone else says. Today, make sure you keep going. Don't quit. You are doing a great job. You can do it.

Questions:

1.   **How can you keep going right now?**

_____

_____

_____

2.   **What seven areas in your life are you going to keep working on?**

_____

_____

_____

JOURNAL:

_____

_____

_____

_____

_____

_____

_____

DAY 108 – TAKE YOUR OWN ADVICE

"It is easier to be wise for others than for ourselves."
– Francois De La Rochefoucauld –

Are you good at giving advice to others? Have you found yourself knowing that advice you give to others applies to you? Do you find yourself resisting your own advice? Maybe you are making excuses for why it's different with you. I am not saying that taking your own advice is easy. There can be a strong disconnect with our own situations while someone else's problems seem really obvious to us. That's fine.

Just remember that you do have solutions for yourself. What you do with your own advice is up to you, but I would recommend you take your good advice. You are smart. You know what to do today. Don't play around with excuses. Just go do the things you already know to do. You will find that your problems start disappearing.

Questions:

1. What do you often tell others?

_____

_____

_____

2. How can you apply that same advice to yourself?

_____

_____

JOURNAL:

_____

_____

_____

_____

_____

DAY 109 – THINK YOU CAN

"If you think you can do a thing or think you can't do a thing, you're right."
– Henry Ford –

You are living up to your expectations. I want you to expect great things. I want you to set your sight on what you can do. All things are possible. If you have an old thought that is no longer serving you, let it go. You don't have to keep focusing on it.

What you think about is what you will bring about. How you think will determine what shows up in your life. Today, you are going to think about things you can do. And today, you will do them.

Questions:

1. **What can you do today?**

_____

_____

_____

2. **What can you do right now?**

_____

_____

_____

JOURNAL:

_____

_____

_____

_____

_____

_____

_____

150 DAYS OF PEACE

"One way to get the most out of life is to look upon it as an adventure."
– William Feather –

I want you to go have fun today. There is nothing stopping you. Find the joy that is waiting around every corner. Make a game out of anything and everything. Don't let the ideas of responsibility or personality keep you from participating in your own life. Why not?

Try something new. Talk to someone you wouldn't normally talk to. Do something that inspires you. If you find yourself waiting in line, make up a game while you wait. Before long you will find yourself smiling and getting the most out of each moment. And then you will look back on your day and say, "What a wonderful adventure I had."

Questions:

1.   What kind of adventure do you want to go on today?

_____

_____

_____

2.   What action will you take in the next half hour to set you out on your adventure?

_____

_____

JOURNAL:

_____

_____

_____

_____

150 DAYS OF
PEACE

"All things are difficult before they are easy."
– Thomas Fuller –

When you have to work to reach a goal you have a greater appreciation when you actually reach that goal. I know that you might be thinking right now how much you want someone to give you what you want. The thought might have crossed your mind once or twice on how much nicer it would be if you didn't have to work so hard. I am all for working smarter, but I also know the value of putting in a good day's work. You know this is true.

Even though you think it would be nice to take the easy way out, sometimes, you also know that you wouldn't be as happy or as thankful once you reached your goal. So, remind yourself that everything gets easier with practice and time. What is hard today, will be a breeze tomorrow. You are right where you need to be. Enjoy yourself.

Questions:
1.   **What are you finding difficult?**

_____

_____

_____

2.   **What are two actions that you can do to practice mastering your difficulty?**

_____

_____

JOURNAL:

_____

_____

_____

_____

DAY 112 – LEARN FROM OTHER'S MISTAKES

"A wise man learns by the mistakes of others, a fool by his own."
– Latin Proverb –

Knowledge is all around you. There are so many people who have done things the hard way and are here to help you learn from their mistakes. You don't have to start from scratch. You don't have to reinvent the wheel. Build on what others have done and what others have learned. To do anything else is foolish.

If you are going to make mistakes (and you will) make new ones. Let the others who have gone before you teach you how to be better. When you let others teach you, you more quickly make your dreams come true. A little humility will go a long way.

Questions:

1.   Who is one person that you could learn from?

_____

_____

_____

2.   What mistake did they make that you can avoid?

_____

_____

_____

3.   How will you avoid their mistake today?

_____

_____

_____

JOURNAL:

_____

DAY 113 – JUST BREATHE AND HAVE FAITH

"Sometimes the best thing you can do is not think, not wonder, not imagine, not obsess. Just breath and have faith that everything will work out for the best."
– Unknown –

Today will be short and sweet. Do you overthink things? By over thinking a situation or problem, you can overcomplicate the solution. Breathe! Nothing more. What will be will be. What is done is done.

Questions:

1.   How can you take more "breaths" today?

_____

_____

_____

2.   What action can you do to keep from obsessing?

_____

_____

JOURNAL: _____

_____

_____

_____

_____

_____

_____

_____

DAY 114 – LIFE IS EVERYTHING

> ## "Life is a child playing around your feet, a tool you hold firmly in your grip, a bench you sit down upon in the evening, in your garden."
> **– Jean Anoullh –**

Life is everything. Life is all around you. Life is anything you want it to be. Don't fall into the trap of defining how life should be or what it should look like. What do you enjoy most? There is life. Look around you right now. The first thing you notice—there is life behind it, through it, and representing it.

You are your life. You make your life what you want by who you speak to and what you choose to interact with. Enjoy yourself and enjoy your life.

Questions:

1.   **What do you relish most about life?**

_____

_____

_____

2.   **What kinds of life do you want to play with today?**

_____

_____

JOURNAL:

_____

_____

_____

_____

_____

DAY 115 – DIFFICULTIES VANISH WHEN FACED BOLDLY

"It has been my philosophy of life that difficulties vanish when faced boldly."
– Isaac Asimov –

I am asking you to face your difficulties with boldness. Don't wait till you feel brave. You will never feel as brave as you need to before you face your fear. You will however, find that you have more than enough courage when you decide to stand up to your fear and look it directly in the eye. Then and only then will you find your difficulties disappearing. You will smile at yourself and think, "What was I so afraid of?"

Questions:

1. What seems like a big obstacle today?

_____

_____

_____

2. What are five ways you can face your difficulty?

_____

_____

JOURNAL:

_____

_____

_____

_____

_____

_____

_____

_____

_____

DAY 116 – YOU ARE NEVER TOO OLD

"You are never too old to set another goal or dream a new dream."
– C.S. Lewis –

Have you been saying to yourself that you don't have enough time? Do you feel like you have missed opportunities and you can't get them back? Dreams have no limits and dreams have no boundaries. That is the great thing about dreams—they are just that—dreams. You are the one who is placing limitations on yourself. You are the one who is saying that it can't be done. Your dream doesn't know the difference between when you were six or one-hundred and six.

Your dream that you have today is limitless and the potential is boundless. I believe in you—now go believe in yourself.

Questions:

1. **What is your biggest dream?**

_____

_____

_____

2. **What is a dream today?**

_____

_____

_____

3. **How can you live part of your dream today?**

_____

_____

_____

JOURNAL: _____

_____

150 DAYS OF PEACE

> ## "I am always more interested in what I am about to do than what I have already done."
> ### – Rachel Carson –

I love a good celebration. It's great catching up with old friends and remembering the fun you used to have. But, don't be content to live in the past, as wonderful as your past might be. Don't let the memories of what was, keep you from the promise of what could be. You are meant to keep moving forward. Go for bigger and better experiences. Yes, be thankful for everything along the way, but don't quit. Keep dreaming and living and experiencing all that you can.

Questions:

1. **What is a new dream you have today?**

_____

_____

_____

2. **What is a new action you want to try?**

_____

_____

_____

3. **Who is a new person you want to interact with today?**

_____

_____

_____

4. **What is a new place you want to go?**

_____

_____

_____

DAY 118 – KEEP YOUR EYES ON THE GOAL

"Obstacles are those things you see when you take your eyes off the goal."
– Henry Ford –

Have you taken your eyes off your goal? Do you find yourself surrounded by obstacles? You need to get refocused. You need to use laser vision and stay fixed on what you want. Have you ever driven off the road? I hope not. But if you have, you will know that once you were off the road, you found yourself facing a bunch of hurdles and obstacles. You no longer were focused on your destination, but you were focused on dogging the danger around you. And most likely, the obstacles brought you to a screeching halt.

Most of the time when we find ourselves off our path, it was unnecessary. We got sleepy or distracted by something that wasn't our goal. We looked away for a few moments or years. Today, I want you to get back to what you were going toward. Renew your vigor. You have much to do.

Questions:

1.   **How have you been a little sloppy?**

_____

_____

_____

2.   **What three actions will you do today to clean up your mess?**

_____

_____

_____

3.   **What six actions will you do to move forward toward your goal?**

_____

_____

_____

DAY 119 – LITTLE THINGS MATTER

"Everything that happens to us leaves some trace behind..."
– Johann Wolfgang von Goethe –

Everything matters. I know it can be tempting to tell ourselves that the little short-cuts that we take aren't really a big deal. You might tell yourself that the speech that is a little unpleasant or the interaction where you were 'less than nice' is ok. "After all," you say, "it's just a little thing." You know that this is not your better Self talking. You know that everything has been leading you up to this moment right now.

You can go and be whatever and whomever you want to be. And, the little moments or the little choices are the vehicles that drive us to what we want and where we want to go. So, be mindful of all things. There are no small moments and there are no small actions. Everything counts.

Questions:

1. **What do you want to create today?**

_____

_____

_____

2. **What little moment will you value when it comes?**

_____

_____

JOURNAL: _____

_____

_____

_____

_____

DAY 120 – CHANGE YOURSELF; CHANGE EVERYTHING

"All you can change is yourself, but sometimes that changes everything!"
– Gary W. Goldstein –

There is always an opportunity for change. You might have told yourself that you can't change or move until something or someone else changes first. You know that this is just an excuse. Yes, sometimes when other events change, it makes it easier for us to change. But, you are not locked into a situation or relationship without a choice.

You can change anything that you want to change. And, the way to change the world around you is to change yourself. It really works. So today, focus on the work of changing yourself. You know what you want to change. You know who you want to be. You know what you want to do. Now go be the change you want.

Questions:

1.   **What do you want to be?**

_____

_____

_____

2.   **What do you want to do?**

_____

_____

_____

3.   **How can you change today?**

_____

_____

_____

JOURNAL:

_____

_____

DAY 121 – BREAKING GOALS INTO SMALL CHUNKS

"Most 'impossible' goals can be met simply by breaking them down into bite-sized chunks, writing them down, believing them, and then going full speed ahead as if they were routine."
– Don Lancaster –

Are you getting overwhelmed? No problem. This just means that you have a really great dream. So, I want you to break down your dream into bite-sized goals. A goal for the year, a goal for each month, a goal for the week, and a goal for today. Now do you believe you can reach these goals?

I know you can. Now go do them. Don't make them special. Make them part of the "normal" events of your day. This way you won't put unnecessary road blocks in front of yourself.

Before you know it, you will have accomplished what you set out to do. Have fun with your dreams. Enjoy your day.

Questions:
1.   **What is your goal for the week?**

_____

_____

_____

2.   **What is your goal for today?**

_____

_____

_____

3.   **What is your goal for the morning?**

_____

_____

4.   **What is your goal for this hour?**

_____

_____

JOURNAL: _____

_____

_____

_____

_____

_____

_____

_____

_____

_____

_____

_____

_____

_____

_____

_____

_____

_____

150 DAYS OF PEACE

"Our greatest weakness lies in giving up. The most certain way to succeed is always to try just one more time."
– Thomas Edison –

Consistency in any area of your life is the key to building momentum. Today, you may find yourself wondering if you should keep trying. I am here to encourage you to do just that—keep going. The moment you decide to give up is the moment you have broken your stride. There is a rhythm and a motion that you have set in place.

Keep practicing who you want to be and what you want to do. There will come a time when everything will fall into place. Until then, the work you have to do today is to keep consciously trying one more time.

Questions:

1.   **How can you encourage yourself today?**

_____

_____

_____

2.   **What have you already succeeded in?**

_____

_____

_____

3.   **What are you going to continue to practice?**

_____

_____

_____

JOURNAL:

_____

_____

DAY 123 – WITHSTANDING HARDSHIPS

"A gentleman can withstand hardships; it is only the small man who, when submitted to them, is swept off his feet."
– Confucius –

You are a strong person. Strong people can endure hardships. Strong people can do more than endure—they can overcome. There is always a moment when you feel like you can't go on—where you feel like giving up or submitting to something or someone that is pushing against you. Take a moment and refocus.

The truth is that you have already overcome many hardships. You wouldn't be here today reading this message if you weren't a person of strength. So remind yourself of what you have done. Remind yourself that you are better than the troubles you see around you. Remind yourself that you can find peace in all things. Move forward today in love and courage knowing that all things are working for you. You are not alone. You are strong.

Questions:

1.   How have you already shown your strength?

_____

_____

_____

2.   What are to actions that will help stabilize you today?

_____

_____

_____

3.   Where can you pull strength?

_____

_____

_____

4. **How can you rejuvenate yourself in this moment?**

_____

_____

JOURNAL:

DAY 124 – CHANGE YOUR MIND

"If you can change your mind, you can change your life."
– William James –

Shift your perspective. There is a message that is in you. There is a light that you have that is uniquely You. However, if you are bogged down in trouble and discouragement the world cannot see what you have to offer. You cannot thrive, grow, and prosper when focused on sadness. There will always be problems, trouble, and decay. But you don't always have to be a part of it. You can see things differently, especially when you feel like there is nothing that you can do. When you feel your hands are tied, and like things are out of your control, then is the time to look inward and find the change in yourself.

Just the slightest change of perspective will shed a whole new light on the subject that has been weighing you down. And most likely, because of that new found viewpoint, you will see answers that you never knew where there. I am not saying that shifting your perspective is easy. In fact, it takes a lot of humility and grace. But I know you can do it. You can find a way to look at your circumstances differently. This will make all the difference.

Questions:

1.   **What is one obstacle you have?**

_____

_____

_____

2.   **What is a different perspective you can have about this obstacle?**

_____

_____

_____

3.   **What are four actions you can take that will reflect your new perspective?**

_____

DAY 125 – WISDOM IS BETTER THAN GOLD

"Wisdom is better than gold or silver."
– German Proverb –

You want the good life. You might want a lot of gold or silver. Who doesn't? Wisdom allows you to get anything you want. Wisdom brings order, balance, and clarity which you need to find your version of gold and silver. So today, don't underestimate the power of wisdom. Take the time to ask the questions you need to ask. Take the time to understand each situation before jumping to conclusions.

Be balanced in your thinking and your emotions. You will find yourself walking down the path of wisdom and doors of opportunity will easily open for you.

Questions:

1.   **What is a wise action you can take today?**

_____

_____

_____

2.   **What needs to be balanced in your life?**

_____

_____

_____

3.   **What are two physical jobs you can bring order to today?**

_____

_____

_____

JOURNAL:

_____

_____

_____

DAY 126 – LEARNING IS A GIFT

"Learning is a gift... Even when pain is your teacher."
– Maya Watson –

Learning is always a gift brought by pain or pleasure. Everything in your life today is an opportunity to learn. Don't run from anything, but ask yourself what can you learn. Take the good and the bad and be thankful for both. Don't take anything personally.

Let go of trying to force your way in every situation. Allow for the learning moments. Listen carefully. Watch everything. Focus on your own area of expertise. Be open for new ideas.

Questions:

1.   What do you want to learn today?

_____

_____

_____

2.   How will you remain open to all teachers?

_____

_____

_____

3.   How will you use the information you gain in your own life?

_____

_____

_____

JOURNAL: _____

_____

_____

"As one goes through life, one learns that if you don't paddle your own canoe, you don't move."
– Katherine Hepburn –

Are you directing your life? Are you waiting for others to tell you what to do? Are you trying to force your ideas on others? You are only in charge of you. You are the only one who can direct your course. No one can do this for you. You cannot do it for others.

So, if you have found yourself floating along, bumping into rocks, and being taken where you do not want to go, then start paddling your own canoe. You will find that it is work, but there will be great joy in knowing where you are going.

Questions:
1. **Where are you going today?**

_____

_____

_____

2. **What are you doing to direct yourself?**

_____

_____

_____

JOURNAL:

_____

_____

_____

_____

_____

_____

150 DAYS OF
PEACE

"If you want light to come into your life, you need to stand where it is shining."
– Guy Finley –

This is simple enough. You cannot receive light while seeking darkness. Your light is what makes you happy. So today, when you find yourself being overshadowed or floundering in darkness, step into the light. There is no reason to continue doing or thinking things that are not helping you. Just stop and do something different.

Release yourself from guilt and obligation. If there is something not good for you then don't do it. If a conversation is bothering you, change the topic. Move yourself away from the problem and towards the solution. You will find yourself having a sunny day.

Questions:

1.   **What is your version of light?**

_____

_____

_____

2.   **What areas can you move into the light?**

_____

_____

_____

3.   **How will you remain in your light today?**

_____

_____

_____

JOURNAL:

_____

_____

"No man was ever wise by chance."
– Seneca –

Wisdom takes practice. There is not a person in this world who just happened upon wisdom. Wisdom is cultivated and cared for. Wisdom grows as you use more of it. Start with the so-called "little things." Ask yourself if you are acting in wisdom.

Use words that are carefully chosen. Don't rush into areas where you have no knowledge. Plan ahead and enjoy the process. Learn what you want to do better and then put your new wisdom into action.

Questions:

1.   What wise choice can you make today?

_____

_____

_____

2.   What wise action will you do?

_____

_____

_____

JOURNAL:

_____

_____

_____

_____

_____

_____

_____

DAY 130 – BE IN LOVE

"You know you're in love when you can't fall asleep because reality is finally better than your dreams."
– Dr. Seuss –

Love is a wonderful thing. Love is a place of complete balance and harmony with yourself and your surroundings. When you find yourself in love with yourself, or others, there is very little that can bother you. Everything seems wonderful and great. What bothered you before isn't that big of a deal.

Today practice love. Find the thoughts that bring you most joy. See everything through the eyes of love. You find that others will reflect back to you more and more love.

Questions:

1.   **What are you in love with?**

_____

_____

_____

2.   **How are you going to show your love today?**

_____

_____

_____

3.   **How are you going to be open to receiving love from others?**

_____

_____

_____

JOURNAL:

_____

_____

DAY 131 – YOUR LIFE IS A MONUMENT

"I made my life my monument."
– Ben Johnson –

Everything you do is creating a monument for yourself. Be mindful today what you are building and why you are building it. The things you do, the words you say, the way you treat people will long outlive you. So, what do you want to create? What do you want to be known for? What do you want to give into the future?

Questions:

1.   **How will you intend to live today?**

_____

_____

_____

2.   **What do you want to be remembered for?**

_____

_____

_____

3.   **What action will reflect the real you?**

_____

_____

_____

JOURNAL:

_____

_____

_____

_____

_____

_____

DAY 132 – DIAMONDS FROM PRESSURE

"The next time you feel slightly uncomfortable with the pressure in your life, remember no pressure— no diamonds. Pressure is a part of success."
– Eric Thomas –

Do you find yourself running from pressure? This is a normal reaction. The right amount of pressure will propel you forward. The right amount of pressure will remove the unwanted things in your life. Without pressure you cannot have a beautifully cut stone. So, allow the rough edges of your personality to come off.

Smooth down the areas where you are a little bumpy. Enjoy seeing what is underneath your hard exterior. I know that there is a beautiful diamond in you. Believe in yourself, allow the process, and have a wonderful day.

Questions:

1.   **What pressure is making you uncomfortable?**

_____

_____

_____

2.   **How can you use that pressure to your advantage?**

_____

_____

_____

3.   **What are two actions today that will allow you to reflect the better You?**

_____

_____

_____

DAY 133 – CHALLENGED TO CHANGE OURSELVES

"When we are no longer able to change a situation, we are challenged to change ourselves."
– Viktor Frankl –

We have talked about this before. Others are not your responsibility. I know this is counter to many beliefs, but the truth is you cannot change others or force them to do something you want. Your job is to change and direct yourself!

Remember this today when you come across a person or situation that bothers you. Instead of asking the person to change, you change. Don't worry about them. They will be fine without you. Focus rather on what you want to be and what you want to achieve.

Questions:

1.   **What do you want to change about you?**

_____

_____

_____

2.   **How can you take action towards that change?**

_____

_____

_____

3.   **How will you commit to continue changing yourself?**

_____

_____

_____

JOURNAL:

_____

_____

DAY 134 – SOLVING PROBLEMS BRINGS PLEASURE

"Unrest of spirit is a mark of life; one problem after another presents itself and in the solving of them we can find our greatest pleasure."
– Kal Menninger –

You are a problem solver. You have the answer in you and around you to bring about a solution to every problem in your life. You are not facing a challenge today that you don't understand and that you can't do something about. So today, ask yourself what solution are you giving. Have fun with finding answers.

Questions:

1. **What solution do you have?**

_____

_____

_____

2. **What action can you take to put your solution in place?**

_____

_____

_____

JOURNAL:

_____

_____

_____

_____

_____

_____

_____

150 DAYS OF PEACE

DAY 135 – YOU ARE HERE FOR A REASON

"We are all here for some special reason. Stop being a prisoner of your past. Become the architect of your future."
– Robin Sharm –

You are here for a reason. This reason is not for you to be held captive to what has happened in your past, but to be the creator and architect of your own life. You can and will construct a new path in your life. Have faith in yourself. Look at what you have already done. Remind yourself of where you want to go. Be kind to yourself and others. Move forward in love.

Questions:

1.   **What new path are you constructing?**

_____

_____

_____

2.   **What makes you special?**

_____

_____

_____

3.   **How are you going to use your gift or talent today?**

_____

_____

_____

JOURNAL:

_____

_____

_____

DAY 136 – LIVE LIKE IT'S HEAVEN ON EARTH

"You've gotta dance like there's nobody watching, love like you'll never be hurt, sing like there's nobody listening, and live like it's heaven on earth."
– William W. Purkey –

No matter what you are doing today, do it for yourself. Don't do it for other people. Do whatever you do because it is what you want to do. And, do each activity with all of your heart. Throw caution to the wind and put your all into the day. Go live your life. You will be glad you did.

Questions:

1. **What will you put your whole heart into today?**

_____

_____

_____

2. **What action will make you happy?**

_____

_____

_____

3. **What activity will you do that you haven't done in a while?**

_____

_____

_____

JOURNAL: _____

_____

_____

_____

DAY 137 - PROJECTION

"If someone tells you, 'You can't', they really mean, 'I can't.'"
– Sean Stephenson –

When someone discourages you from your dreams, realize that it is a reflection of their unfulfilled dreams. Don't take anything they say personally. As you live your life and fulfill your dreams, you will have all the encouragement you need. You don't need others to tell you that you are doing a good job.

You know you are doing great. Look how far you have come and look at your bright future ahead of you! And, as you grow in confidence, you can then turn around and encourage others.

Questions:
1.   **What have you accomplished that you are proud of?**

_____

_____

_____

2.   **How will you remind yourself throughout the day that you are doing great?**

_____

_____

_____

3.   **How can you encourage someone today to keep going?**

_____

_____

_____

JOURNAL: _____

_____

DAY 138 – YOU CAN ACHIEVE IT

"If you can dream it, then you can achieve it. You will get all you want in life, if you help enough other people get what they want."
– Zig Ziglar –

We are all looking to make our dreams come true. There is no thought that you have that you cannot make happen. You have people around you who need a solution that only you have. And in turn, remember that they have an answer to your question. We all connect together.

Have an open mind to how your dreams can dovetail into the other's dreams. Don't be afraid to collaborate with anyone who has a mutually beneficial goal. There is enough of everything for everyone.

Questions:

1.   **Where can you collaborate with someone else?**

_____

_____

_____

2.   **How can you both benefit from working together?**

_____

_____

_____

3.   **How will you reach out to them today?**

_____

_____

_____

JOURNAL:

_____

_____

150 DAYS OF
PEACE

"No matter what the situation, remind yourself, 'I have a choice.'"
– Deepak Chopra –

You always have a choice. You are not a victim. You can always be better than your situation. You might not like the choices you have, but you do have a choice. And, taking the best choice in every moment will lead you to better and better situations. Trust yourself. Trust the process and have faith that you can lead the life you always wanted.

Questions:
1.   **What is the best choice for you today?**

_____

_____

_____

2.   **How will you put that choice into action?**

_____

_____

JOURNAL:
_____

_____

_____

_____

_____

_____

_____

_____

DAY 140 – NO NEED TO WORRY

"I've had a lot of worries in my life, most of which never happened."
– Mark Twain –

Worrying is not going to solve your problems. Worrying will not make your life better. To worry is to loop around a subject with no answers. Worry comes from a fear that has no resolution. Most of your fears have very little basis in current reality.

Most of us carry fears that were true at one point but that don't match up with who we are and where we are going. So, you need to ask yourself if the fear you have is current, or is it from the past. Remember that you are no longer that person. You have grown and changed. So too have your circumstances. Align your thinking with thoughts that are solution-based. Dismiss those thoughts that do not serve you.

Questions:
1.   **What is your fear today?**

_____

_____

_____

2.   **Is your fear valid?**

_____

_____

_____

3.   **What action places you out of fear and into solutions?**

_____

_____

_____

JOURNAL:

_____

_____

150 DAYS OF PEACE

"If opportunity doesn't knock, build a door."
– Milton Berle –

I love this quote. You will have many doors come across your path. Some are others' doors, some are yours. Some doors you are just going to have to build yourself. Don't always wait for someone else to show you a door or to open the door for you. Sometimes you have to start from the ground up. Your opportunity will come over and over to you. Take a "no" as a direction to the next "yes". Easy your mind and then get to work.

Questions:

1. **Have you knocked on all the doors available?**

_____

_____

_____

2. **What is a door that you should build?**

_____

_____

_____

JOURNAL:

_____

_____

_____

_____

_____

_____

_____

_____

150 DAYS OF PEACE

"A friend is someone who knows all about you and still loves you."
– Elbert Hubbard –

You want true friends. You want friends that will stick with you through the good times and the bad times. However, like attracts like. So are you being the friend that you want to have? It is simple. Do to others those things that you want to be done to you. You are wonderful. Let people see who you really are.

Questions:

1.   **How do you like to be treated?**

_____

_____

_____

2.   **Are you treating others the way you like to be treated?**

_____

_____

_____

3.   **How can you be a good friend today?**

_____

_____

_____

JOURNAL:

_____

_____

_____

_____

150 DAYS OF PEACE

"There are two ways of spreading light; to be the candle, or the mirror that reflects it."
– Edith Wharton –

There are two ways of spreading light. You are the light or you are the reflection of the light. Today look for light. Maybe it is the light that is within you, or you find light in other people. Then, I want you to spread some of that light around. If you can't find a bright spot on a certain subject, get around someone who can. Reflect the light they have.

Questions:
1.	**How can you shine your light?**

_____

_____

_____

2.	**How can you reflect other's light?**

_____

_____

_____

JOURNAL: _____

_____

_____

_____

_____

_____

_____

_____

Day 144 – YOU'LL FIND A WAY

"If you really want to do something, you'll find a way, if you don't, you'll find an excuse."
– Jim Rohn –

You get what you want. When you find yourself saying that you can't have what you want, you are really saying you don't want to do the work it takes to get it. So ask yourself if you really want what you say you want. If you do want something, then do the work to get it. If you find the work is not worth it, then stop saying you want it. Keep your focus clear and your speech consistent with your focus.

Questions:

1.   **What do you want?**

_____

_____

_____

2.   **How are you getting what you want?**

_____

_____

_____

JOURNAL:

_____

_____

_____

_____

_____

_____

_____

_____

DAY 145 – GO WITH THE FLOW

"I may not have gone where I intended to go, but I think I have ended up where I needed to be."
– Douglas Adams –

How did you end up here? Have you ever asked yourself that question? I think we all have. Realize that you are 'here' because you need to be. Everything that you have around you and every experience that you have is necessary for your growth and your success. Don't complain about anything. Take what you can use, and find the joy along the way. Keep a good perspective and enjoy your day.

Questions:
1.   **What are you thankful for?**

_____

_____

_____

2.   **What are you happy about?**

_____

_____

_____

JOURNAL: _____

_____

_____

_____

_____

_____

_____

_____

_____

DAY 146 – DESIRE TO SUCCEED

"The will to win, the desire to succeed, the urge to reach your full potential... these are the keys that will unlock the door to personal excellence."
– Confucius –

Excellence can be achieved in everything that you go through. It is really simple. Follow your instinct. You know what you want. You know who you really are. Go follow those ideas.

Questions:

1.   What is your instinct telling you?

_____

_____

_____

2.   What action are you going to take to follow your true self?

_____

_____

_____

JOURNAL:

_____

_____

_____

_____

_____

_____

_____

_____

_____

"Hope is a waking dream."
– Aristotle –

You might be in the future hoping your dreams will come true. I want you to be in the here-and-now. I want you to realize that you are living your dream presently. This is your happily-ever-after. What you do in this moment is what life is all about. Take advantage of all the resources that are now here for you. Don't put things off until tomorrow. This is your day—this is your moment—this is your life. Right here. Right now.

Questions:

1.   **How are you living your dream right now?**

_____

_____

_____

2.   **How can you enjoy this moment?**

_____

_____

JOURNAL:

_____

_____

_____

_____

_____

_____

_____

_____

DAY 148 – IT'S ALL ABOUT PERSPECTIVE

"We don't see things as they are, we see them as we are."
– Anais Nin –

There is no way around it. You are looking through the world from your particular perspective. This is a good thing. No one can see things quite like you can. No one has the answers that you have. No one is just like you.

However, this also is a reminder that we can have a perspective that doesn't serve us. When you find yourself around things you don't like, take hope. All you need to do is shift perspectives, and the things around you will either disappear or become less of a problem. You are that powerful. So, use the gift that is You. Don't take things so seriously. Find the viewpoint that brings you the most joy. You have control. See what you want to see.

Questions:

1.   **What do you want to see?**

_____

_____

_____

2.   **How will you align your thoughts to what you want?**

_____

_____

_____

3.   **What action will you take that reflects your shifted perspective?**

_____

_____

_____

JOURNAL:

DAY 149 – THE DIFFERENCE IS ATTITUDE

> **"There is little difference in people, but that little difference makes a big difference. The little difference is attitude. The big difference is whether it is positive or negative."**
> **– W. Clement Stone –**

Sometimes the things that make the biggest impact on our lives are the little things. And, the little thing that I am talking about today is your attitude. What is your attitude like today? You know when you are grumpy. You know when you are full of life. Sometimes, you can go either way.

So, take a moment and adjust yourself. Go meditate, pray, breathe, sleep, or go for a jog. Maybe all you have to do is think of something funny or sweet. But, whatever your method is for getting attitude adjusted—go do it. It is not worth going through the whole day mad at the world. This gets you nowhere fast.

We are all alike in many ways. But, we can be very different because of what we choose to do in each moment. Today, I know you want success. Today, you want to feel good and be happy. Adjust your attitude to reflect what you want.

Questions:

1.   **How is your attitude?**

_____

_____

_____

2.   **What can you do to keep your attitude positive?**

_____

_____

_____

JOURNAL:

_____

_____

DAY 150 – HAVE POSITIVE EXPECTATION

"An attitude of positive expectation is the mark of the superior personality."
– Brian Tracy –

Expect the best from your life. I don't care what your personality is, I know you want to be happy. I know you want to feel worthy and loved. I know you want to see your dreams come true now and in the future. So, expect for all of this to happen.

Don't go about your day looking for trouble. Don't get yourself into a mind frame of fear.

Have confidence that life is working out for you and that things are only here to enhance who you are.

Questions:

1.   **What great expectation do you have today?**

_____

_____

_____

2.   **How can you find joy even before your expectations are met?**

_____

_____

_____

3.   **What positive action will you take today?**

_____

_____

_____

JOURNAL:

_____

_____

Conclusion

৪০

Congratulations on completing *150 Days of Peace – Devotional & Journal*.

You did it!

I trust that the journey has been a transformative one that has helped you develop some new skills, gain greater insight, and create new habits in various areas of your life. But, the journey doesn't need to stop here.

Be sure to keep this devotional close by and reference it as often as you need to. I would even suggest getting another copy of this devotional and go through the process again. You will only reinforce the growth you've obtained. Once you have completed the process again for the second time, compare your answers and notes from the first, and you'll be surprised with the remarkable progress you have experienced.

I'd love to know how this book has changed your life and what new habits have been formed in your life.

How has this book changed your relationships, your health, and your outlook on life?

As our journey transitions to its next stage, I'd like to leave you with a few thoughts.

Celebrate the results of your work.

The progress you have experienced throughout the last couple of months has come as a result of your consistency and commitment to your personal growth. Continue growing and discovering areas of your life that you want to improve.

As always, I stand with you as a partner in your personal growth. Keep up the great work!

150 DAYS OF PEACE

DEVOTIONAL & JOURNAL

OVER 4 MONTHS of daily exercises and
encouragement that creates a life of
abundant peace, **clarity**, & **harmony**

For more books and programs,
visit **CalvinWitcher.com**

*Subscribe to our mailing list and
join our online community*

Notes

Introduction

[i] Maltz, Maxwell. Psycho-cybernetics: A New Way to Get More Living Out of Life. N. Hollywood, Calif: Wilshire Book, 1976. Print.

[ii] Lally, Phillippa. "How Are Habits Formed: Modelling Habit Formation in the Real World - Lally - 2009 - European Journal of Social Psychology." Wiley Online Library. N.p., 16 July 2009. Web. 1 Sept. 2016.

Quotes

All quotes are taken from the following, unless otherwise unknown:

Goodreads
http://www.goodreads.com

BrainyQuote
http://www.brainyquote.com

Holy Bible
The Holy Bible. NY: Nelson, 1953. Print.

Meet The Author

CALVIN WITCHER is an Author, Teacher and Spiritual Crusader that has coached international teachers, doctors, therapists, business professionals and individuals seeking clarity. Known for his bold and integrative approach to spirituality, he calls all to freedom and the soul's highest calling.

Calvin is the host of his self-help show on YouTube, and his podcast, Expect Great Things, which debuted in the top 30 Spirituality video podcasts on iTunes. He is a sought after thought-leader, conference speaker, and workshop facilitator in the fields of philosophy, spirituality, and personal development and has been featured in Success Magazine.

As a gifted counselor and speaker, the core of Calvin's message is "helping others find clarity through challenge, crisis, and change". Transcending socioeconomic and denominational barriers, his message resonates among people from every walk of life.

With a faith undaunted by the task at hand, this husband, father, and mentor is the prophetic voice to a progressive generation. Today, as a much-in-demand speaker and proclaimer of inclusivity and interfaith, he continues to fulfill his mission to radically heal and transform lives.

Calvin Witcher is available for speaking, teaching, consulting and counseling. For media inquiries, ideas for collaboration and more information, **please visit CalvinWitcher.com**